# STRAIGHT TALK ABOUT SEX

by Barry Chant

Whitaker House
PITTSBURGH and COLFAX STS., SPRINGDALE, PA 15144

STRAIGHT TALK ABOUT SEX

Copyright © 1975 by Barry Chant

Additions and Revisions
Copyright © 1977 by Barry Chant
Printed in the United States of America
ISBN: 0-88368-078-5

*All rights reserved. No portion of this book may be used without the written permission of the publisher, with the exception of brief excerpts in magazine articles, reviews, etc. For information, address Whitaker House, Pittsburgh and Colfax Streets, Springdale, Pennsylvania 15144.*

All Bible quotations are from the Revised Standard Version, copyrighted 1946, 1952, © 1971, 1973.

# CONTENTS

*Foreword*
*Introduction*

## PART ONE

1. The stage is set.................................................... 9
2. Tamar—whose beauty was more than skin deep................................................. 15
3. Amnon—who made himself sick ......................... 25
4. What are you? A man or a mouse? ..................... 31
5. Partners in grime ................................................. 37
6. It's just an old, old story..................................... 43
7. How near can you get? ....................................... 61
8. Folly or fun?........................................................ 65
9. The eternal triangle............................................. 75
10. No trespassing..................................................... 85
11. Till death do us part........................................... 105
12. Getting it all together......................................... 115

## PART TWO

13. The purpose of sex ............................................. 128
14. Celibacy: some advantages of the single life......................................................... 137
15. Masturbation....................................................... 142
16. Homosexuality: some questions and answers ........................................................ 148
17. Famous last words............................................... 164
18. Things you probably want to know................... 170

# FOREWORD

Here is a book called "Straight Talk About Sex." Any book with this title has three things to live up to: It has to be straight, meaning the shortest distance between my heart and God's; it has to be a talk, someone speaking directly and closely to me; and it has to be about sex, a subject more talked about and less understood than almost any other.

Barry Chant has done this, and done it well. This little book goes high on my list of things said simply, realistically and Biblically to a great need. I know Barry, and he knows what he's talking about. As a scholar, he's thought about it. As a teacher, he makes things clear. As a pastor, he makes it practical. As a man, he's lived it.

If you want a book on sex that avoids the questions, hedges on the answers and misses the point completely—get something else! "Straight Talk About Sex" is all it claims to be.

Winkie Pratney
*Author of Youth Aflame and
Doorways to Discipleship*

# Introduction

"What do you think of that book?" I asked a group of young people. The book in question was a new paperback on the Christian attitude toward sex.

"Do you really want to know?" they answered.

There was something about the way they said it that confirmed my own fears.

"No," I answered. "I don't suppose I do."

It was obvious that the book had not impressed them. For although it claimed to be a manual for Christian youth, to help them overcome sexual difficulties, it failed dismally. In simple terms, it committed the worst of all crimes for young people—it was unreal. It failed to come face to face with practical issues. It hid behind pious platitudes and proof texts. If anything, it made things worse than they were before.

"Why don't *you* write a book?" someone asked me.

"Me? Oh, no. There're too many books on the subject already." And I proceeded to tell these young folks the titles of a couple of good ones that I knew.

But they were persistent. They had heard me speak on the subject and felt that what I had said was worth sharing with others as well.

"I'll tell you what," said one of them. "I'd buy it."

So I was sure of selling one copy at least!

That was several years ago. Since then, I have spoken to a number of youth and church groups on the subject. I have counseled individuals. I have read further. And I have discovered three things.

First, there is a keen enthusiasm among young people to hear a frank and open Christian presentation of the issue that is usually of first importance to them.

Secondly, there is a general reluctance on the part of many pastors and parents to deal with the subject head-on. They tend to hide behind generalities—generalities which normally leave young people frustrated, but afraid to ask the questions they really want to ask.

Thirdly, there is a general ignorance of healthy, Biblical, Christian attitudes toward sex. There are, it is true, many books on the subject but somehow they are not being widely read.

So I have, after all, decided to go into print. I think I have some things to say that I haven't seen presented in quite the same way elsewhere. And I hope that one more book on sex will increase the chances of young folks finding some answers. Here then, for better or worse, is the book.

If you like it, I might even sell two copies!

P.S. By the way, all the stories told in this book are true, but some details and all the names have been altered, for obvious reasons.

# PART ONE

## 1. The Stage Is Set

If you think that this book is going to be just another spiel by an adult telling young people what to do, then you are absolutely right. This is exactly what it is. But before you close it and look for an Archie comic, just read on a little bit, anyway. You never know what you might find out!

The teenage years are usually the most vital and exciting in life. And one of the things that makes them most thrilling, and at the same time the most troubling, is the awakening of sexual capacity and desire.

I have been told that there is a form of microscopic life in which there are 26 different sexes! We have enough trouble with just two! But the point of this book is to show that it is possible for sex to be enjoyed to the full, and yet contained within the standards laid down by the Bible, the Word of God.

That doesn't mean that all I am going to do is preach. I believe that intelligent young people need to be told more than just "the Bible says." You want to know *why* the Bible says what it says. You have a right to an explanation. This is what I am going to try to do.

There is a story in the Old Testament which sets out the whole picture very well. You'll find it in 2 Samuel chapter 13.

There are five major characters in the story. First, and most important of all, is
   **Tamar**—a beautiful virgin
Then there is
   **Amnon**—Tamar's half-brother, a virile youth
The other characters are
   **Jonadab**—a crafty fellow, and Amnon's companion
   **Absalom**—Tamar's big brother
   **David**—the elderly king, now rather out of touch

In order to save you time and trouble, I have set out the story in full right here.

Now Absalom, David's son, had a beautiful sister, whose name was Tamar; and after a time Amnon, David's son, loved her. And Amnon was so tormented that he made himself ill because of his sister Tamar; for she was a virgin, and it seemed impossible to Amnon to do anything to her. But Amnon had a friend, whose name was Jonadab, the son of Shimeah, David's brother; and Jonadab was a very crafty man. And he said to him, "O son of the king, why are you so haggard morning after morning? Will you not tell me?" Amnon said to him, "I love Tamar, my brother Absalom's sister." Jonadab said to him, "Lie down on your bed, and pretend to be ill; and when your father comes to see you, say to him, 'Let my sister Tamar come and give me bread to eat, and prepare the food in my sight, that I may see it, and eat it from her hand.'" So Amnon lay down, and pretended to be ill; and when the king came to see him, Amnon said to the king, "Pray let my sister Tamar come and make a couple of cakes in my sight, that I may eat from her hand."

Then David sent home to Tamar, saying, "Go to your brother Amnon's house, and prepare food for him." So Tamar went to her brother Amnon's house, where he was lying down. And she took dough, and kneaded it, and made cakes in his sight, and baked the cakes. And she took the pan and emptied it out before him, but he refused to eat. And Amnon said, "Send out every one from me." So every one went out from him. Then Amnon said to Tamar, "Bring the food into the chamber, that I may eat from your hand." And Tamar took the cakes she had made, and brought them into the chamber to Amnon her brother. But when she brought them near him to eat, he took hold of her, and said to her, "Come, lie with me, my sister." She answered him, "No, my brother, do not force me; for such a thing is not done in Israel; do not do this wanton folly. As for me, where could I carry my shame? And as for you, you would be as one of the wanton fools in Israel. Now therefore, I pray you, speak to the king; for he will not withhold me from you." But he would not listen to her; and being stronger than she, he forced her, and lay with her.

Then Amnon hated her with very great hatred; so that the hatred with which he hated her was greater than the love with which he had loved her. And Amnon said to her, "Arise, be gone." But she said to him, "No, my brother; for this wrong in sending me away is greater than the one which you did to me." But he would not listen to her. He called the young man who served him and said, "Put this woman out of my presence, and bolt the door after her." Now she was wearing a long robe with sleeves; for thus were the virgin daughters of the king clad of old. So his servant put her out, and bolted the door after her. And Tamar put ashes on her head, and rent the long robe which she wore; and she laid her hand on her head, and went away, crying aloud as she went.

And her brother Absalom said to her, "Has Amnon your brother been with you? Now hold your peace, my sister; he is your brother; do not take this to heart." So Tamar dwelt, a desolate woman, in her brother Absalom's house. When King David heard of all these things, he was very angry. But Absalom spoke to Amnon neither good nor bad; for Absalom hated Amnon, because he had forced his sister Tamar.

Before we look at some of the issues raised in this story, I would like to add one further passage from the Bible. It is a promise—a promise that it *is* possible to live a pure life—a life that is free from lust and unbridled passion.

This passage is not a negative, restrictive command telling you what *not* to do. It is a promise telling you what you *can* do through Jesus Christ.

> "His divine power has granted to us all things that pertain to life and godliness, through the knowledge of him who called us to his own glory and excellence, by which he had granted to us his precious and very great promises, that through these *you may escape from the corruption that is in the world because of passion, and become partakers of the divine nature.*"
> (2 Peter 1:3 and 4)

Now let's read on, and make our escape!

## 2. Tamar—Whose Beauty Was More Than Skin Deep

*"Now Absalom, David's son, had a beautiful sister, whose name was Tamar."*

Tamar was beautiful. Now, not all girls have the same problem! So they use all sorts of methods to improve. Lipstick, powder, eyebrow pencil, nail polish, hairspray, deodorant, moisturiser, demoisturiser, shampoo—not to mention all the other things they do to get themselves in good shape!

The result is usually pleasant for both fellows and girls. And I'm all in favor of girls being as beautiful as possible. I think girls are marvelous inventions!

But, having said that, it must be pointed out that there is a difference between beauty and suggestiveness. Girls can dress themselves so that the result is either one of those two. A girl can be beautiful without being suggestive; and she can be suggestive without being beautiful.

I led a discussion on Christian dress with a youth group once. It was going fairly well until one of the fellows, named Andy, spoke out.

"I'd like to say that the way some of the girls dress, I find it hard to keep my thinking clean. They stir me up inside."

A number of things happened in very quick succession. First of all, I was stunned by the lad's frankness. I knew that even though I had exactly the same problem when I was his age, I would never have dared to confess it in front of a mixed group—or in front of *anyone*, for that matter!

Secondly, the girls immediately burst into a silly giggle—especially the younger teens who were present. They obviously thought that what he said was a joke.

Thirdly, in spite of the girls, the fellows all kept very serious and silent. It was clear that Andy was speaking for all of them, although they weren't prepared to say so!

There was only one thing to do. I moved in immediately with a stern rebuke to the girls which, I might add, took them all rather by surprise. I commended Andy for his frankness and explained to the girls that what he said was absolutely true. I was a bit hard on them, really, but I wanted them to get the message.

I explained to them that beauty can have two kinds of effect. For instance, you can look at a beautiful sunset and be struck by its splendor. But you don't want to possess it. You can't take hold of it or do anything with it, except perhaps steal it with your camera.

On the other hand, you may see a beautiful roast chicken. If you are hungry, you don't want to just stand there and look at it! You want to take hold of it, possess it, consume it, be satisfied with it.

This is the kind of feeling that a girl who dresses provocatively can create. She creates in the male mind not just a feeling of admiration, but a desire for possession, for satisfaction. And this is an entirely different matter.

Now, I understand that most girls don't realize this. They are duped by the fashion designers into thinking that boys like looking at them just because they are attractive. This is only part of it. Dress which suggests nakedness is highly provocative—in fact, even more so than nakedness itself. You may ask, "What's wrong with nakedness, anyway? Didn't God create the human body? Isn't it a beautiful thing?"

At the time of writing, this has become a particularly lively question. There are beaches throughout the world that have been set aside for nude bathing. People everywhere are arguing both for it and against it. And a lot of people can't see anything wrong with it.

If we look into the book of Genesis, however, we find one or two very interesting things about nakedness. The most important of all is this: You remember that after Adam and Eve sinned, the first thing they did was to make clothes out of fig leaves? And then when God asked them, "Who told you that you were naked?" they couldn't answer? For *no one* had told them! They just *knew*. (You can read the story in Genesis chapters 2 and 3.)

What had really happened was that through sin they had become *spiritually* naked. The protective righteousness with which God had surrounded them was removed. And because they were spiritually naked, they also felt physically naked. So they tried to cover up.

To blatantly display the naked body—or to dress in such a way as to *suggest* nakedness—is virtually an act of defiance against God. It is saying, in effect, "We have no need of covering, God. We're OK. We don't need You at all!"

So, girls, for the sake of the fellows, and in respect for the holiness of almighty God, be careful how you dress.

I hesitate to name any particular fashions, because by the time this is in print styles might be completely different! But some things can be said. I have been told, for example, that the mini-skirt was originally designed specifically for its suggestive qualities. And there are other fashions which fall into the same category.

In the end, the simplest formula is: necklines up, hemlines down. Plunging necklines and rocketing hemlines are explosive for the fellows. Girls, for the boys' sake, try to be beautiful without being provocative!

Now, I know there are problems. In some places it's almost impossible to buy clothes that are decent. To maintain Christian standards, it may be necessary to make your own clothes. You may have to accept the fact that there are some clothes in your wardrobe that you will never wear again. If so, it will not be the first time that Christians have been called to suffer inconvenience for the sake of Christ.

I spoke on this theme at a youth meeting once on a very hot night. After the meeting, I noticed that one young girl was wearing a cardigan. She was obviously uncomfortable, but did not take it off.

The next day, when I was about to leave that town, her mother came to thank me for what I had said to the young people. Her daughter had been pestering her to make a "halter" top and she had, in fact, been wearing a borrowed one the previous night. But after the talk, she told her mother that she didn't want one any more. And that's why she had been wearing the cardigan.

The girl was standing right there, so I turned to her and apologized for causing her to be uncomfortable the night before.

"That's all right," she said. "I'm glad that you spoke as you did. I want to do the right thing."

Previously, she just hadn't understood.

In speaking of halter tops, girls, I would like to add one more thing—*don't go braless!* Such suggestiveness can be a great temptation to the fellows around you and that is really unfair to them.

The following letter was written to me by a young man who was engaged to be married. Both he and his fiancée were Christians. I think that it speaks for itself:

> "I am continually amazed today at the suggestiveness of girls. Joanne, my fiancée, and I were discussing the seriousness of the slipping away of standards—especially within the church. The fashion influence seems to be invading the lives of Christian girls as strongly as it is invading the lives of non-Christians.
>
> "Standards? Where are they? At a recent youth meeting we were amazed at the way the girls presented themselves—not only in the area of fashion, but in movement, gesture, speech and action.

"Our conclusion was that fashion and its trappings have infiltrated the church to a sharp degree, and something needs to be done very quickly to make young people more aware of their responsibility to God, to others and to themselves in this regard.

"For a long time, Joanne has considered saying a lot of things to some of the girls, in spite of the risk of being labeled prudish or square. So far, she has kept silent.

"As you know, I work in a department store as a window dresser, so I'm exposed to the whole range of passing fancies. The other day, Joanne was examining the fashion department, but she couldn't find one decent garment. It was not because of a lack of stock, either. Most of the styles and cuts were impossible to consider. I realized then that it must be hard for a girl to find something suitable without being suggestive.

"I would like to say something about fashion designs. It seems to me that the motives, patterns and tones of many garments have a satanic touch! They seem to reflect an offbeat approach, if that is the word, that indicates Satan's subtlety in the fashion world.

"Is it too much to suggest that these designs have a part in gearing young people to accept more readily the occult and other similar practices? There may be overtones of brightness, gaiety and verve—but are these, in fact, tools of a system that is conditioning the public slowly to accept the weird and whacky as the norm?

"The cut of many clothes today suggests lewdness. It is not just the color or the fabric, but the way they are being combined that is the problem.

"Men, also, need to be very careful about the clothes they buy today.

"I guess I've been challenged more recently about this because of the nature of my work. If what I have suggested is true, then am I assisting to promote the very fashions I am criticizing? This troubles me at times, but God has His reasons for me being there, and I hang on to that."

Too often, Christian girls allow the world to dictate their standards of dress. Placing popularity and the approval of their peers at the top of their lists of priorities, they allow God's standards to come second or third—or even lower than that.

Christian young people need to face the solemn reality that they do not live in a totally Christian society. Like the first Christians, they live in a heathen, godless community. But, they are a people set apart. Their standards are very different. And this includes standards of dress.

In some cases, it goes deeper than dress, too. Some girls are provocative and suggestive regardless of what they wear! Their very manner seems to accentuate their sexuality. I don't suppose this applies very often to Christian girls. I hope not, anyway. In most cases, I think, Christian girls do not intend to be suggestive. If they are, it is usually because they are simply unaware of the effect their appearance can have on the fellows.

Tamar, the Bible says, "was wearing a long robe with sleeves, for thus were the virgin daughters of the king clad" (2 Samuel 13:18). In other words, there was nothing provocative or revealing about the clothes she wore. It wasn't her dress that got her into a mess with Amnon.

Girls, you may have to face social pressures, perhaps even scorn from school—and work-mates. But it's worth it. If you don't dress carefully, don't lay all the blame on the fellow if you get into trouble.

You may have asked for it.

## 3. Ammon—Who Made Himself Sick

*"And Amnon was so tormented that he made himself ill because of his sister Tamar."*

Being lovesick is a popular concept with fiction writers. From Chaucer's ailing Troilus, to Shakespeare's mooning Romeo, languishing lovesick heroes have drifted over the pages of literature. And it still happens today.

I remember when I was about 16, I had fallen for a girl who didn't return the affection. I was sitting very quietly at the table one night, when my Dad said to me, "What's the matter with you? Lovesick?"

"Yes," I replied. "I am."

He nearly fell off his chair laughing.

My love sickness was instantly cured!

Dad went on to give me some sound advice, the

only part of which I remember was, "There are plenty more fish in the sea." Heartened by this previously unrealized, but obvious revelation, I immediately looked around for further fishing grounds.

In my day, however, the pain of love sickness was that even if the affection was returned, we were taught that there would be no sexual fulfillment outside of marriage (although not everyone thought the same way). Today, many more people feel differently about waiting for marriage. And, of course, Amnon felt differently, too.

Today, Amnon's philosophy has become accepted on almost every side. It is essentially hedonistic. In other words, if something gives you pleasure, if you feel like doing it, then go ahead—do it. If you enjoy it, it's probably all right.

A good test of such a philosophy is to push it to extremes. Does it *always* apply? If you feel like murder, for instance, is it all right to go ahead?

In all these things, however, the battleground is really our minds. What we finally end up doing, we have already done in our thoughts. This is where battles are either won or lost.

Now Jesus Christ had something very specific to say about this. Look at His words:

"You have heard that it was said, 'You shall not

commit adultery.' But I say to you that everyone who looks at a woman lustfully has already committed adultery with her in his heart." (Matthew 5:27-28)

You see, the act is only the expression of the desire. What you would *like* to do indicates what you really are. Amnon wanted not only to admire Tamar, he wanted to possess her. He wanted to have sexual union with her. And this is why he made himself ill. It was his real nature coming out—*even before any act was committed.*

Purity and morality, then, are *matters of the mind.* So Jesus says that he who would *like* to commit adultery with a woman has already done so!

The expression that Jesus uses here is very interesting. In the Greek text it reads literally: "Everyone who looks at a woman *with a view to* lusting after her..." It is clear that the Lord is not talking about a fellow who turns a corner and is suddenly confronted with a slashing girl of goodly figure who makes his heart skip a beat and his stomach jump. That happens to every man. What he is talking about is the chap who has that experience and then turns back to continue looking, to feed his desire, to titillate his passions.

The first look is often unavoidable; the second look may be the adulterous one. It is those men who ogle a girl, who gaze upon her with lust in their eyes who commit sin.

I feel sorry for young men today—especially those who are trying to maintain a pure outlook. They are surrounded on every hand by a philosophy which declares that sexual expression is normal between any consenting couple. They are confronted every day with newspapers, magazines, advertisements and television programs which operate on a hedonistic level (if it feels good—do it!). Even where no particular moral outlook is expressed, as such, the general field of reference is one of looseness and so-called freedom. Even worthy films and magazines are spoiled by advertisements or snippets of licentiousness.

What fellows—and girls—need to realize is that each is attracted to the other sex for different reasons. To a fellow, the first attraction is basically visual. The form of the female body is essentially stimulating to the male mind. Without knowing anything about a girl, a fellow may find her attractive just by looking at her. And this, of course, is why many advertisements, book covers, films and magazines feature the female form.

A woman, on the other hand, does not always find the male form sexually stimulating. A man who is physically attractive may promote feelings of strength, warmth and security, more than sexual desire. The female body responds more readily to touch. Thus, there are more erogenous areas on a woman's body (i.e. areas that respond to touch) than there are on a man's. And this is the way God has arranged it. The whole process of courting, wooing and loving depends to some extent on these physical factors.

However, it must be added that much of that same advertisement that tantalizes a man often serves to deceive a woman into believing that her need for love and security will be fulfilled by sexual involvements outside of marriage. Thus, advertising makes it immensely difficult for young Christians of both sexes.

But difficulty has never been an excuse for giving in! To the young man, Timothy, the Apostle Paul wrote:

> "Take your share of suffering as a good soldier of Jesus Christ...
> Shun youthful passions and aim at righteousness..."
> (2 Timothy 2:3, 22)

## 4. What Are You? A Man or a Mouse?

Problems are usually balanced by privileges. This is how it is with people. We have the problems of facing moral issues; but we also have the privilege to make our own decisions. Even wrong decisions.

Now, this is in strict contrast with the insect or animal world. The lower down the biological scale you go, the less freedom of choice there is.

Even the "highest" forms of life like dogs, horses and apes have really a very limited ability to learn, compared with humans. Certainly they are not troubled by moral issues.

Thus, in the animal realm, sex is purely functional. Its purpose is reproduction. It is no more than a biological urge, dependent on natural impulses and the season of the year.

With humans, however, sex is far more than this. It is essentially an expression of love and commitment.

People have the marvelous privilege of learning, of loving and of choosing; a privilege unknown to any other form of life. However, this very freedom to learn what we will, to love whom we will, to choose what we will also lays us open to the possibility of learning and choosing evil, and of loving self more than anything else.

This is why thought life is so important. Here decisions are made. Here choices are decided. Here destiny is determined.

I once received a letter from a young man who was having difficulties with his thought life because of what he read. It is a common problem. Probably, there is hardly a fellow reading this who has not pondered, at some time, over the pages of a magazine or book in which photos of naked women appear.

This young man had been doing just that. This is what he wrote:

> "After a time, I realized that I wasn't satisfying anything within me. Far from relieving desires that I felt, I was simply stirring them up. I was, in fact, becoming more frustrated. And with this there was a horrible emptiness.
>
> "I put the book away and looked for my Bible. I was browsing through passages that I had read before that I thought might help me. I remembered that there was something in the book of

Proverbs and finally found Proverbs 5:18-20. It says:
'Why should you be infatuated my son,
with a loose woman,
and embrace the bosom of an adventuress?'
I thought about that and realized that in spite of my own inner conflict, I would never even think of having relations with a prostitute or an adventuress. So the passage didn't seem to fit my case.

"But suddenly, I saw the connection between this and what Jesus had taught in the Sermon on the Mount. Adultery could be a matter of either the *body* or the *mind*.

"What kind of women allowed themselves to be photographed in this way? Would 'adventuress' be a good description? I realized that it would and that I had, in fact, been 'embracing the bosom of an adventuress' with my eyes.

"The whole thing took on a new light. It could no longer be considered an inoffensive thing. It wasn't just a harmless diversion.

"I saw it as the weakness and selfishness that it was. So I took the book and burned it—just to make sure I wouldn't be able to indulge in that way again! Then, soon after this, I was able to spend a couple of days in fasting. This further discipline helped me to bring my whole body under control.

"But the real victory was in my mind. I had to control my thoughts."

What this fellow wrote is right on. It fits in perfectly with the words of Paul who gave the following very practical advice:

"Take every thought captive to obey Christ." (2 Corinthians 10:5)

Who is master of your thoughts?

In another place, Paul declares, "I will not be enslaved by anything" (1 Corinthians 6:12). Here is the cry of the liberty of the children of God! Christ has set you free. Do not allow anything to captivate you again.

After a service one night where I spoke on Christian marriage, a young man named Jim asked to talk with me. He told me that he had been involved in homosexual activities. For eight months he had kept clear of this, but a week ago he had fallen again. I encouraged him in the usual fashion to confess it to God, to accept His forgiveness, and then to go on in his victory. But somehow talking to him was like talking into a dead telephone.

So I asked Jim some further questions.

"How did you come to be involved anyway?"

"I was approached in a public toilet."

"Well, Jim, if I were you, I'd steer clear of such places as far as possible."

"Oh, but that's not the only place you can be approached. I've had it happen to me in movie theaters."

"Well, Jim, stay away from theaters."

"Oh, I couldn't do that, Pastor. I see every film that comes to town. I'd commit suicide if I didn't go to the movies."

"Well," I answered, "that is your problem, isn't it? How do you expect to stay clean if you see every film that comes along? You can't go to R- and X-rated films and expect to be unaffected."

"They don't affect me at all," he argued. "In fact, I also watch—" and here he named some television programs which are based heavily on the sex theme. "But," he went on, "these things don't stay in my mind."

"Oh, come on, Jim. Of course they do. As long as you feed your mind like this, you'll naturally be stimulated and aroused. What about your Bible? Do you ever read it?"

"I never read anything."

"What about midweek meetings?"

"Oh, I went once, but I didn't like it."

And so it went on. It turned out that this boy never did anything other than what he wanted to do. His whole life was an undisciplined shapeless jelly that flowed into whatever mold was available.

Take every thought captive to obey Christ. Remember that Amnon *made himself* sick. He could have controlled his lust. But he didn't. And the tragedy that followed was the result.

## 5. Partners in Grime

*"But Amnon had a friend whose name was Jonadab... and Jonadab was a very crafty man."*

Have you ever noticed that when you want to do something wrong, there's always someone around to help you do it? But when you want to do what's right, you often stand alone?

It's always been that way.

In this case, when Amnon was becoming increasingly frustrated because it seemed "impossible for him to do anything to Tamar," Jonadab came to his rescue.

It is pretty clear from the story that Jonadab had already made a few conquests, and probably had a trail of broken hearts behind him. He was only too ready to lead Amnon into trouble.

It would be interesting to have a survey done of all the people who first took a drink, or a cigarette, or a

drug, or who first committed fornication (sex outside of marriage), because there was someone egging them on to do it.

So strong is the desire to be one of the crowd, to maintain the respect of one's equals, that some folks will do anything rather than lose it. Don Lonie, popular speaker to high school and college groups, once said, "A fellow starts smoking to prove that he's a man: and twenty years later he tries to stop smoking to prove the same thing."

Do you know why your companions want you to do *their* thing? It's not for *your* sake: it's for *theirs*. No one ever asks you to sin because they really think it will do you good. They do it because it makes them feel better to have a companion sharing their weakness with them.

You see, if you work with a group of fellows or girls who are taking drugs, for example, and you don't take them, your behavior shows theirs up. Or, if they like to swap the latest depraved joke, and you don't, they probably won't like it. You don't have to say a thing. Just the way you are makes them uncomfortable.

Of course, they may respect you for it. But they'd still feel more comfortable if you'd join in.

This is more or less what happened in Jesus Christ's own experience. He once said,
  "If I had not come and spoken to them, they

would not have sin; but now they have no excuse for their sin."
(John 15:22)

The result was that they hated Jesus, and because they could not get Him to join in their wicked ways, they tried to get rid of Him.

It will be the same with you. As long as you determine to be different, you will be respected, but disliked. If, however, you show any sign of going their way, you will have friends in a moment only too willing to show you how you can share their sin.

People make jokes about being lonely in heaven, but having lots of friends in hell. That's all right until you face the reality of it.

I remember hearing a monologue about an old alcoholic whose wife remained true and faithful to him right through the years of unhappiness.

But then old Will lay on his deathbed. His wife stood there and looked at him without a tear in her eye.

"I'm not going to call in a preacher for your funeral, Will," she said. "I'm going to get all your friends from the bar to gather round. They can conduct your service. They're more your kind."

Suddenly, Will realized that he was about to die and his only friends were those who didn't have any idea of how to live, let alone how to die. The shock sobered and *revived* him.

He got up, repented, and lived his remaining years as a God-fearing man!

I don't know if that story's true, or just an old tale. But there is a truth behind it. When you really need friends, it's good to have friends of the right kind. In the meantime, if necessary, it's better to stand alone.

> "Therefore take the whole armor of God,
> That you may be able to withstand in the evil day, and having done all, to stand.
> Stand therefore..."
> (Ephesians 6:13-14)

Therefore, stand!

## 6. It's Just An Old, Old Story

So Jonadab and Amnon worked out a scheme. Amnon was to pretend to be sick—which didn't require much acting at the time—and he was to request that Tamar come and tend to his needs. Then he would lure her into his bed.

The ridiculous thing about the whole scheme was that it was all unnecessary. Amnon and Tamar both had the same father—King David—but different mothers. According to the laws of those days in Israel, they could have married if they had wanted to. All Amnon had to do was seek permission, wait till the appointed time, and proceed with a wedding.

But this was not his aim. Amnon didn't want to get married. His purpose was sexual gratification only. And that couldn't wait.

So he and Jonadab worked out a "line" on which they hoped to catch poor Tamar.

In this, of course, there was nothing new. Men had used similar lines before, and they have used them since. No doubt they will continue to use them in the future. So at the risk of supplying the fellows with some ideas, I am going to expose a few popular lines—in order that the girls may be warned. And then, just to even it up, we'll look at some bait cast out by the girls, for it's not entirely a one-way affair!

I remember when there was a serious gas shortage in my home city because of an industrial dispute in which truck drivers went on strike.

A daily newspaper carried a cartoon showing a couple in a car on a deserted country road, under the full moon.

"I'm out of gas," said the fellow.

"And I'm on strike," said the girl.

What follows is of the same nature.

(1) The "nobody loves me" line

I knew of a young girl who fell victim to this one. When she was on shift work, a married man sometimes took her home. Gradually, he unfolded a sad story of an unhappy home, of a wife who didn't understand him, of the increasing frustration of being neglected and unloved. In this case, it took months for anything to develop, but finally the girl, Betty, in genuine compassion for him, was embracing him, until eventually she had intercourse with him.

Ultimately, the inner conflict which this set up brought her to a point of breaking down, and she confessed the whole thing to her pastor.

She is now overseas and happily married to a young man who was prepared to forgive and help her to remake her life. But it took a long time for the scars to go away. And the marriage nearly didn't come off at all.

In this case, both Betty and the man concerned actually fell into a trap which neither envisaged in the first place.

But many has been the time when right from the start the "nobody loves me" approach has been used unscrupulously for selfish ends. And it's not only the fellows who use it. More than once a girl has tried the same approach on her man to break down his standards.

The whole thing rests upon a distorted idea of what love really is. Paul tells us that "love does not insist on its own way." Or, to use the old version, it "seeketh not her own." Love concentrates on giving, not receiving.

The best answer for those who feel unloved is to give love. And for those who fall victim to this "line" the best answer is to say, "I love you enough to respect you and to give myself to you—but only as God allows."

## (2) The "aren't you lucky" line

This is the character who makes you feel as though going out with him is the greatest thing that's happened to you since you got your first Christmas presents.

"You know, I think you're okay, and I'd like to take you out, but I have to take Sylvia to the movies on Tuesday, and I've promised to meet Joan at the Pizza Bar on Wednesday, and then Friday's booked up too—Anne wants me to meet her parents, and then I'm always busy on Saturday. But look, we could do something on Thursday."

Immediately, you think, "If I don't go out with him Thursday, I might not ever get to go out with him."

So you say, "Yes," and then late on Thursday night when he expects you to respond to his sexual advances, and you say, "No," he tells you that he certainly won't be taking you out again. And knowing how much in demand he is, and how pretty Sylvia is, and that Joan probably gives in to him, you think, "If I don't cooperate, I might lose him altogether."

So you give in to what is actually an ugly, one-way experience that leaves you cold, unfulfilled and guilty.

And he never takes you out again, anyway.

Listen, girls. If he's so much in demand, let him go! A man who's prepared to keep so many girls interested when he's *unmarried*, is not likely to change when he *is married*. To try to net that kind of fish is to catch an octopus. You'll reap a life of sorrow. It's not worth it.

### (3) The "if you loved me you would" line

This is probably the most popular line used. How can you say "No" if you love him? How can you refuse something wonderful to someone you love? It's hard to resist.

Or is it? There's a very simple answer really.

When he says, "If you loved me you would," you say, "If you loved me, you wouldn't!"

Again, we ask, what is love? Is it taking, or is it giving? Does a fellow who loves a girl want to abuse her—the object of his love?

Someone once wrote: "A boy declares his love so that he can have sex; a girl has sex because she wants love."

I think that is very near to the mark. The two things should not be confused. Sex is not necessarily love and love is not necessarily sex. Only under the right conditions can they go together. A boy who asks for love needs to ask himself first if all he really wants is sex. If he is honest, he may change his whole approach.

### (4) The "everybody does it" line

This is another very popular approach, and it's gaining more victims daily.

But again, the answer is very simple: "Everybody doesn't. I don't."

Any dead fish can go along with the tide. It takes a good, live, strong fish to swim against it. There's no merit in doing what everybody does. Strength of character is often shown in standing alone.

Amnon, for example, could have taken note of Eleazar, one of his father's three mighty men. Once, when all of his companions fled from the battlefield, Eleazar refused to withdraw. He fought till he was weary and "his hand cleaved to the sword." But he was victorious and the Philistines fled in disarray. And "the Lord wrought a great victory that day" (2 Samuel 23:9-10).

He might have said, "Everyone is running. So will I." But everyone did not retreat. Eleazar didn't.

### (5) The "we're getting married anyway" line

This is another popular excuse for fornication. Statistics indicate that 90 per cent of the girls who marry, having already had sexual experience, did not have it the first time with the fellow they married. Clearly, many of them who once agreed that "we're getting married anyway"—didn't.

I remember one fellow whom we shall call Bill. He was engaged to be married. Both he and his fiancée were Christians. But they were not walking very close to the Lord.

When I met him, although the wedding date had been set and all the plans made, the wedding was called off. The engagement was permanently broken.

"What do I do now?" he asked.

"What do you mean, Bill?"

"Well, I thought we were going to be married. And..." He paused. I completed the sentence for him.

"And you had sexual relations with her."

"Yes, Pastor, I did."

"And now you wonder how you will face the future?"

He nodded silently.

He knew that he would be sexually frustrated, and even more, he wondered how he would now relate to another girl should there be one.

I could multiply similar stories. The hardest part is always when the next prospective partner comes along. Sooner or later they have to know. The risk is that the second one might be lost because of the folly of taking things for granted with the first.

You may not think that risk is very high. I assure you that when you are faced with the possibility, it is.

I can recall one lass who had to face this problem. She had fallen in love with a young fellow, but she was not a virgin.

"Should I tell him?" she asked me.

"Yes, Marion, I think you should."

"But when? Do I have to tell him now, Pastor? What if we break it off?"

I understood her distress. I prayed for guidance and believe that the answer I gave her was a result of that prayer.

"Marion, you do not need to tell him unless he proposes. But then he must know."

A few weeks later she came to me again. She was

very upset.

"Pastor, he proposed last night," she told me.

"What answer did you give?"

"I didn't give him any answer," she replied. "I put him off."

I knew why, but I waited for her to continue.

"Pastor, what if I tell him and he decides not to marry me?"

"That's a risk you will have to take, Marion. If he truly loves you, he will still accept you."

It was not long before her boyfriend proposed again. And this time she agreed—but only after she had "something to tell him."

He heard her out in silence. Then, they sat for a very long time together. He loved her, but he had loved her without knowing this.

He took her home without saying much, and he hardly slept that night. But the next day he knew what he would do.

"I still love you," he told her. "I have been pretty upset about what you told me, but I reckon that if the Lord has accepted you and forgiven you, I'd better do likewise. I still want you to marry me.

Will you?"

You can imagine the rest for yourself!

But it could have been different. The only really safe way is to keep yourself until that day when there is no need for fear at all.

One Monday morning my telephone rang very early. I was still in bed, but staggered gropingly for the phone. On the line was a young fellow named Dennis. He had heard me speak on Christian marriage the previous evening at a crowded rally in a city theater. He told me his story.

"I'm 19 years old, and I'm going with a girl who's 17. We want to get married, but Helen's parents, who are on the verge of separation, won't give permission.

"We have become involved sexually, anyway. And the other day, someone told us that the legal side is only a bit of paper and that in God's eyes we are already married.

"So we thought it was all right to go on having sex. But after hearing you last night, we're not sure."

"Dennis," I said, "the Bible has a name for what you're doing. It's fornication. And you'd better stop."

There was a silence on the line, so I continued.

"Furthermore, Helen should obey her parents, and you should both do what thousands of other Christian kids have done—wait. Finally, you should get in touch with your pastor and talk it over with him."

I guess I could have been a lot more tactful. But when you are summoned from bed and you're still half-asleep, it's not always easy to remember the niceties of life. So I gave it to him straight.

He thanked me, promised to see his pastor and hung up. I don't know what happened. But I do know that this was just another example of young people being deceived into thinking that you can give sin a sugar coating and call it by another name.

Even if you *are* planning to marry, there is still one thing to do. Wait.

It won't hurt you.

### (6) The "don't be frigid" line

Too often words are used out of context, with the wrong meaning and in an unfair way. This is a classic example.

To call a girl "frigid" is to suggest that she is incapable of sexual response. On rare occasions, this may be true. There are sometimes psychological factors stemming from childhood or teenage experience which do produce frigidity.

In the majority of cases, however, any girl who is tenderly treated and shown genuine love is capable of full sexual response. To expect her to be like this, however, in the back seat of a car at a drive-in theater, or in conditions where she is afraid of being discovered or put to shame is both unrealistic and unworthy.

Any girl has a right to be "frigid" in such circumstances. She needs the shelter, protection and warmth of a secure, loving relationship—which only marriage can provide.

To accuse her of frigidity outside of this is unkind, unloving and selfish. No girl should accept it. It is an insult of the worst kind.

### (7) The "I won't take you out again" line

This is a kind of variation of both the "everybody does it" and the "aren't you lucky?" approaches. It suggests that if you want to be taken out you have to do what everyone else does and do it while you've got a chance.

"All the other girls I've taken out have obliged," said one fellow.

"Then why do you need me?" came the reply.

My heart grieves for the many Christian girls that

I have known who have thrown their lives away for a worthless fellow in desperation, to avoid being left on the shelf.

They reach the ripe old age of about 22 and can't sleep at night for fear of becoming old maids. So when a fellow finally turns up they will do anything to keep him.

On the other hand, I can remember another girl who was approached by a young man, but who knew that he was not the right one. She was impatient to marry, but she sought my advice.

"Do you know that when the devil wants to stop you from getting God's best, he often slips a second best in front of you to lead you astray?" I asked her. "Maybe God has someone special just round the corner, if you will only wait."

She waited, and less than three months later, the right man came along!

Better to be single a few more years, if necessary, than spend a lifetime of unhappiness.

I know how difficult it is for Christian girls. Often you are in a small church where the field is pretty narrow. You know that you should have a Christian man, but what if there isn't one?

And then comes Joe or Fred or Mac. And he's a steady type, good job, good-looking. Well, his moral standards aren't quite the same, but after all, it would be terrible to be a spinster forever.

And so you give in.

I think of one girl who did this. No Christian men were eligible, it seemed. And so when an attractive non-Christian came along, she married him.

Today she is divorced, living alone, caring for her children and having to work for a living.

Now, there are a few *girls* who want to take the lead, of course. And they have a few tricks of their own. Here are a couple.

### (1) The "what sort of man are you?" line

You will notice the similarity between this and a couple of the male approaches. Just as no girl wishes to be thought frigid, so no man wishes to be thought incapable or impotent.

Nothing hurts more than an affront to the male ego.

But as for the fair sex, so for the stronger. Don't let yourself be tricked into folly. What sort of man are you?

The sort of man who respects a girl?

The sort of man who realizes that there is an obligation to sexual relationships—an obligation to provide a secure environment for them?

The sort of man who is prepared to stand up for God and what is right?

The sort of man who can't be tricked into a phony love?

If that's the sort of man you are, then you have nothing to worry about.

## (2) The "don't stop now" line

This is another line that works both ways. It can be used by both fellows and girls.

Roger was a young man who preached once in a while at a little suburban church. Wendy was an attractive girl who used to attend there, and he invited her out a few times. She was barely a Christian when Roger first met her, and had come from a pretty loose environment. She had been involved in sexual relationships frequently.

But now, she was trying to turn her back on all this. Roger led her on spiritually, and she became enthusiastic for God. At the same time, the relationship between the two became stronger.

Soon, they were showing their affection with kissing and embracing. While Roger was a mature

Christian for his age, and fairly strong in his self-discipline, this deepening relationship awakened all the old desires in Wendy.

One night she took his hand and placed it on her breast. He removed it, but she kept guiding it back, until finally he left it there.

He made no attempt to go any further, but she was deeply aroused. Finally, whispering, "Don't stop now," she tried to lead him further.

Suddenly, he realized what she meant, became frightened and withdrew from her embrace altogether. He went home soon after, guilty for what he had unwittingly done; and she sat a long, long time awake, frustrated and also guilty. Both of them were so perplexed that the relationship soon broke up.

The mistake was not that they stopped when they did, but that they did not stop sooner. They allowed themselves to go too far in the first place, and thus both nearly fell into a trap.

### (3) The dress line

Of course, the most popular line used by girls—and often used unwittingly—is provocative dress. This has already been discussed, so I will not dwell on it further here.

Let me just say, again, that given the clothes that

some girls wear, you can't always blame a fellow for taking liberties. There is often literally an open invitation.

## 7. How Near Can You Get?

*"So Tamar went to her brother Amnon's house, where he was lying down."*

It is interesting to ask where Tamar went wrong.

Everything she did seemed innocent enough. As far as she knew, Amnon was genuinely sick. Furthermore, her father, the King, instructed her to go to Amnon's house. To bake cakes for her ailing brother was a charitable thing to do. Even to take the cakes into him was normal enough. He was supposedly too sick to get up for himself.

In fact, it was Tamar's very sweetness and innocence that got her into trouble. Had she been more knowing she would have become suspicious as soon as Amnon ordered all the servants to go out, leaving the two of them alone. But that's often the way. It's not the deliberately promiscuous girls who find themselves in difficulties. It's those who have no intention of doing wrong who are caught. The others take precautions.

In simple terms, all that Tamar did wrong was to be where she shouldn't have been.

Did you ever hear the story of the man who applied for a job as a coach driver in the old days? In answer to the advertisement he joined a waiting line at the manager's office. As the various applicants came out they told the others what to expect.

"He doesn't say much," they said. "All he does is ask you how close you can drive a coach-and-six to the edge of a cliff."

"What did you say?"

"I said I could get within five feet."

"Wasn't that good enough?"

"Doesn't seem like it. I didn't get the job."

A couple of others came out. But even three feet wasn't close enough.

When the man in question went in, he was confronted with the same test:

"Well, my man, how close could you drive one of my coaches to the edge of a cliff?"

"Well, sir, if I was driving one of your coaches, I wouldn't go near a cliff at all, sir."

He got the job!

There is no virtue in seeing how close you can go to danger and still escape. Sailing close to the wind might be all right in some quarters, but in moral issues, it's potentially disastrous.

Do you remember the Bible story of Jacob's son, Joseph? When he was in the respected position of overseer in the household of Potiphar, one of the king's officers, Potiphar's wife took a liking to him and tried to seduce him. But Joseph steadfastly refused. In fact, the Old Testament writer says,

> "And although she spoke to Joseph day after day,
> he would not listen to her, to lie with her *or to be with her*."
> (Genesis 39: 10-11)

Notice those last words. He would not even *be* with her. When she finally did catch him by surprise, grabbing onto his coat and attempting to draw him into bed, Joseph ran off, leaving his garment with her. In revenge, she turned the coat into false evidence that Joseph had tried to assault her. But even being near Potiphar's wife that day was not Joseph's fault. He had gone into the house simply "to do his work."

As far as Joseph was concerned, he kept as far away from danger as possible.

In contrast to this, read the later story of Samson (Judges 14-16), who time after time allowed himself to go to the cliff edge. Finally, he went over.

But back to our story:

And Amnon forced Tamar down on to his bed, and in spite of her protests, raped her.

It's a sad story, but one that in various degrees has been repeated a thousand times in a thousand places. Many a beautiful girl has been spoiled by making the same simple mistake.

Now, let's be realistic. Most of the young men reading this book have no intention of forcing a girl against her will. And most of the girls have no intention of luring a fellow beyond his intentions.

What happens most often is not usually planned. The two get together. They begin to kiss, to embrace, to fondle one another. Each time it is easier to go a little further than the time before. And finally, although neither of them planned it that way, they finish up having sexual intercourse.

But, the situation need never arise. The solution is simple. To avoid falling into temptation: **Always be where you can be interrupted.**

As your relationship progresses, be alone by all means. You don't want the whole world listening while you talk of your love, your plans for the future, your delight in each other. But be alone in a place where there is always the possibility of interruption.

*Always be where you can be interrupted.*

In other words, stay well away from the cliff. (And my wife adds; "And the beach!")

## 8. Folly Or Fun?

*"Tamar answered him, 'No, my brother, do not force me...do not do this wanton folly.'"*

Some time ago, I wrote an article on Christian involvement in moral protest. In the course of the article, and in an attempt to set the proper balance, I wrote, "Sex is fun."

I received a protesting letter from one elderly reader about this statement. "It were better left unsaid," he wrote. I respected his opinion and answered his letter, but the essence of my response was, "Well, isn't it?"

Sex *is* fun. It's marvelous fun. And that's why it's so attractive. But you've got to play according to the rules. If you don't, your fun will turn to folly.

Said Tamar to Amnon, "Do not do this wanton folly."

Says Chant to you, "Likewise."

In fact, it sometimes seems to me that we preachers have done a lot of harm by condemning sex outside of marriage as sin, neglecting to emphasize how very foolish it is! Don't get me wrong. *It is sin.* But it is also folly. And this is what I am heading at here.

Some young people today are saying this sort of thing:
"It's not timing that matters, it's meaning. What does it matter whether we have sex before or after marriage, as long as we love each other?" This is a question that I hope the rest of this part of the book will answer.

**What a Shame**

Tamar gives us our first answer. To Amnon she said in effect, "If you go through with this, you will be a fool and I will be ashamed. And where does one go to hide one's shame?"

What she said proved true. What grief and tragedy is packed into these words:
> "And Tamar put ashes on her head, and rent the long robe which she wore; and she laid her hand on her head, and went away, crying aloud as she went."

A century ago, people used to talk about losing one's virginity as a "fate worse than death." Today's "enlightened" generation laughs at that. What husband expects his bride to be a virgin these days?

I can tell you a few. I was one, for a start. And I believe that most Christian men have similar expectations. I wish I could share with you the grief that I have seen in the lives of a couple of young men and women who had to climb over this obstacle to reach the altar. The agony of the girl who had to tell the man she loved that if she accepted his proposal, he must know that he was not the first. And the agony of the man who had to decide whether he was prepared to accept the girl on this basis. It doesn't seem real until you are faced with it. Then it is only too real.

Those who do not know Christ may find these few lines hard to understand. But those to whom Jesus Christ is a living and personal Savior will understand what I mean. Sin is never pretty.

To those of you who have had sexual experiences and now come to Christ, of course, the past is forgiven and done with. Any Christian man or woman must accept you as a virgin in Christ. But this is still not always easy.

You may not understand it, or believe it, but what Tamar said is still true. "Where could I carry my shame?"

**All the way?**

One popular expression for sexual intercourse is "going all the way."

It's an interesting expression because it's completely misleading. It may be accurate in a physical sense, but it's completely inaccurate in a spiritual sense.

Physically, I suppose it must be conceded that intercourse is the climax of sexual expression, and thus going all the way.

But spiritually, emotionally and psychologically it is not even going half the way. Indeed, it is less than a third of the way, a quarter of the way.

Male-female relationships are very complex. It is not a simple matter of following a biological urge on an animal level. Sex is but a part of a total relationship. There are, for example, three basic areas of personality: the spirit, the mind and the body. Consider the following diagram:

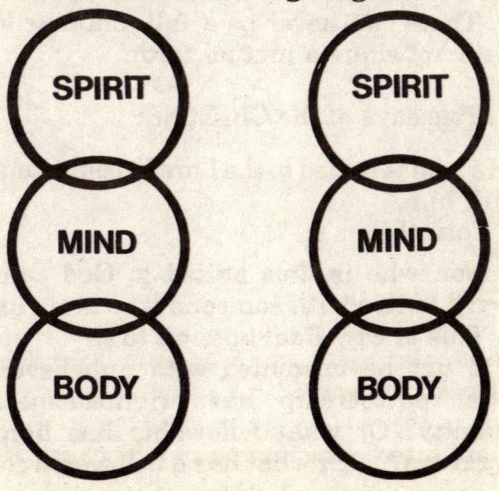

The two piles of circles represent two people. (The pretty one is the girl!)

Now, if they are to share a total relationship, they will do it on all three levels.

**Spirit**

First, and most important, is the union of spirit. This means, essentially, a sharing of spiritual experience. For a man and a woman to be truly one means that they must be one in spirit as well as everything else.

One of the first things that two young people who are attracted to each other should find out is where each stands spiritually. For a believer, for example, to seek union with a non-believer is absolute folly. There can never be a full union as long as they do not share a mutual faith.

The Bible says of the Christian:

> "He who is united to the Lord becomes one spirit with him."
> (1 Corinthians 6:17)

A person who is thus united to God cannot be properly united with someone who is cut off from God. This is why Paul goes on to say:

> "Do not be mismated with unbelievers. For what partnership have righteousness and iniquity? Or what fellowship has light with darkness?... Or what has a believer in common

with an unbeliever?..."
(2 Corinthians 6:14-15)

Spiritual union is plainly impossible in such a case.

Any Christian fellow or girl who knowingly enters into a contract with a non-Christian is committing the most blatant foolishness—and disobeying God in the bargain. And any non-Christian who tries to marry a Christian is being equally foolish.

Conflict will develop almost immediately and it is a conflict that will probably increase. What is going to be done with the children? What will happen on Sundays when one partner wants to worship and the other wants to go fishing? When you are confronted with problems, and you need to pray together about them, what will you do? And so on.

Spiritual union is of first importance.

But having said that, it must also be pointed out that it is possible to have a spiritual union without anything else. Union in this area is not going "all the way" either. It is only a part of a total male-female relationship.

**Mind**

There is also the union of two minds.

A perfect relationship between two people includes

some measure of agreement in the area of the intellect. This is rarely perfect, of course, but there needs to be something there. You need to have some interests in common.

If you like reading and he can't stand reading; if you enjoy music and she abhors music; if you prefer mountain holidays and she loves the sea; if you enjoy company and he is a recluse—you will have problems. You may survive one or two of these differences, *but you must agree on some things*. Even if you agree on everything, however, you still haven't gone "all the way."

**Body**

Then there is physical union.

It should be clear by now that this is but one part of a total relationship. To be united physically *only* is certainly not to go "all the way."

In fact, from the point of view of time alone, physical union is but a fraction of a total union. Even if you were to make love every day of the week, you would still be spending only about one-twentieth of your time in physical union.

Union on other levels, however, continues all of the time. Indeed, sexual intercourse is but an expression of the deeper union that exists.

It's not the whole relationship; it's but a part!

Now you might argue, "Well, then, if we are united spiritually, and intellectually and socially, why do we have to wait until we marry to be united physically?"

I have already pointed out the unhappiness experienced by some who have acted on this basis, and then later separated, full of regret.

But there is more yet to say than this.

Read on!

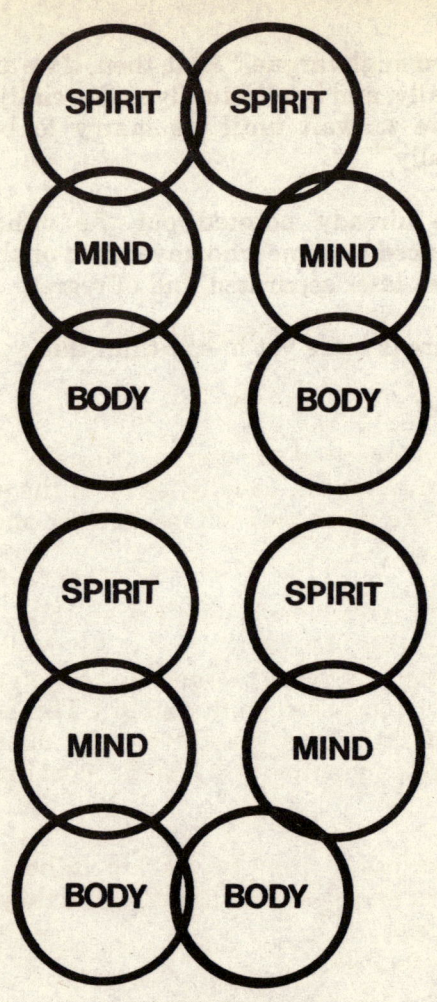

**Examples of partial
—and inadequate—
union**

## 9. The Eternal Triangle

You have heard of the eternal triangle, no doubt. It's the description usually given of the situation that occurs when two fellows fall for one girl; or vice versa.

But there is an older triangle than this—and one which is truly eternal. To find it, we must go back to the very beginning of time. We are going to hear what God has to say on the subject. This is, in fact, the first thing that God ever said about male-female relationships; and it is the most important.

Listen:
> "Therefore a man leaves his father and his mother and cleaves to his wife, and they become one flesh."
> (Genesis 2:24)

There are three essential parts to this verse. They can be depicted as three points of a triangle. Like this:

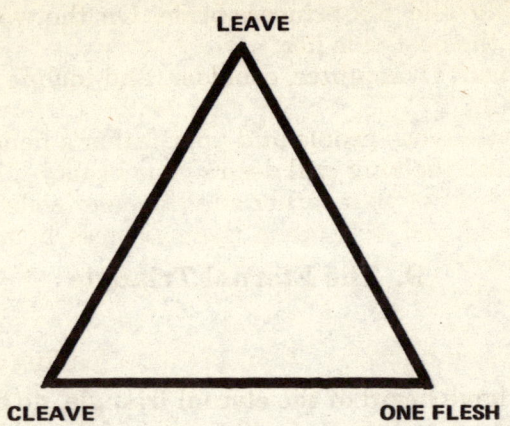

## Leave

Before a couple can be joined in marriage, they must leave the old family relationship. There must be a parting with the old way of life.

When I was a teenager, there was a popular song called, *"I Never See Maggie Alone."* The words told of a poor youth who was in love with a girl named Maggie. But every time he tried to see her, or take her out, her family always came, too. So he took her out in a row boat, and alone at last, in the silence of the quiet stream, he began to talk of love. When suddenly,
  "There was her father, her mother,
  Her sister and her brother,
  O! I never see Maggie alone!"

There is a beautiful love song in the Psalms about

a King and his princess-bride. On the wedding day, the poet tells her:
"Hear, O daughter, consider, and incline your ear;
Forget your people and your father's house;
 and the king will desire your beauty...
Instead of your father shall be your sons;
 and you will make them princes in all the earth."
(Psalm 45:10, 11, 16)

Total commitment, then, involves leaving one's parents and making a new start.

**Cleave**

After leaving, comes cleaving.

To cleave means simply to stick. Once you have made the choice, you are stuck with it!

Seriously, though, this is really the most important part of any relationship. A satisfactory relationship can only be built on *commitment*. *This is of vital importance.*

Commitment is expressed in the marriage service. Here is an example:
"I, John, take you, Mary, to be my wedded wife,
to have and to hold from this day forward,
to share my faith in Christ,
and to make my home with you,
for better, for worse,

for richer, for poorer,
   in sickness and in health,
   to love and to cherish,
   till death do us part,
according to God's holy Word.
Before God, I pledge you my faithfulness."

Similar vows are made by the bride.

If you look at them closely, you will see that the essence of these vows is commitment. Here are two people promising to be true to each other as long as they live, and pledging before God to be faithful to each other.

Unfortunately, today marriage is too often a convenient arrangement, made by two people who have no intention of keeping such vows if the going gets rough. They treat marriage like buying a new car: if it starts to act up, trade it in on a new model.

But, marriage is not just an economic or social contract. It is an agreement between two people to be true to each other; to stick together; to be permanently joined.

There can be no substitute for this.

Shirley was a Christian girl who was very active in the work of the Lord. Then, mysteriously, she began to be absent from meetings from time to time, her absences becoming more extended.

One of her friends came to see me. She told me that Shirley was involved with a fellow who had been a Christian, but who had drifted away from Christian activities. Shirley loved him, but felt ashamed about it because of the lad's spiritual condition. So she stayed away from church.

Shirley was attending some meetings where I was teaching, and so I spoke to her one night.

"Shirley, I understand you have been missing from church a bit lately."

As soon as I said this, she turned her back on me and began to walk away.

I called to her quickly. "Shirley, you may not want to talk about it, and I won't force you to. But don't don't just turn away from me. Perhaps you need to share it with someone?"

She responded immediately and turned back with an apology. "I'm sorry, Pastor. I'll talk about it if you like."

"Well, then, Shirley. What's the trouble?"

She told me about the young man. Then she dropped a bombshell.

"I'm going to live with him in two months' time."

"What do you mean?"

"Well, he has an apartment, and we're going to live there together."

"You're getting married?"

"No. We're just going to share the same apartment."

"But why not get married first?"

"I want to. But I don't know if Milt wants to or not. And it's not my place to ask him to marry me. I'm the girl. It's the man's part to propose."

"Have you talked together about marriage, Shirley?" I asked.

"No. I think Milt should be the one to bring it up."

I was astounded, and told her so.

"Do you mean to say that you can talk about living together, you can make plans about moving into an apartment, you probably have already had intercourse," (she nodded faintly) "and yet you can't talk about marriage! Come on now, Shirley."

"But we feel that we have a beautiful relationship going now. We don't know what it will be like in the future, so we just want to enjoy it now without committing ourselves."

"Do you know what I think?" I replied. "I think

your fellow knows only too well what he's doing. He doesn't want to marry you because he's afraid of being tied down. He wants to leave a loophole. To have a way out. You're being treated like a toy that might be thrown away in a few weeks, spoiled and broken."

We left it there. Shirley went away thoughtful.

Then one night she came up to me looking very happy.

"Guess what happened last night!" she said. "Milt proposed to me! We're going to be married."

She was radiant, her eyes shining. I hoped that Shirley's boyfriend truly loved her and that everything would work out well. I didn't know Milt at all, so whether he would make a good husband, I couldn't say. But at least he was prepared to commit himself to her and accept his responsibility.

One young fellow said to me once, "Marriage is only a bit of paper. And then it ties you down. It's a bind. Love is enough to hold people together. You don't need marriage."

My reply was, "If you really love a girl, why are you afraid of being legally committed to her?"

A truly committed marriage provides a foundation on which to build. In my marriage, a very happy one of seventeen years at this writing, we have found that our mutual commitment has made us strong. Far from being a rope around our necks, it has been an anchor in time of storm. When we have faced difficulties, we have tackled them from this viewpoint, "We are *committed* to each other, therefore we *have* to work things out."

And we have.

Our commitment has taught us that there is no need to run away from problems or to give up in the face of diffiuclty. Because we are committed, we can use this very commitment as the strong foundation on which to stand firm.

**One Flesh**

In the third and last part of the verse, God talks of sexual union.

It comes after cleaving. And this is where it belongs. For sexual union is only fully meaningful in the context of a *wholehearted commitment*.

I think that girls especially appreciate this. They need a secure, loving environment for such an intimate, personal relationship. Often, they will give in anyway, but it is frequently against their real feelings. Deep down they want security.

One young man told me of several of his workmates who were each living with a girl. All of them boasted that marriage was unnecessary. But within two years, all were married. The girls, in every case, realized that what they had was second best. They needed a stable, secure relationship.

It is not enough to simply talk of having mutual interests, spiritual union and therefore sexual union. With this must also come strong commitment—dedication to each other. And this is only fully expressed in marriage.

To summarize then, the oldest statement on marriage known to man teaches that it takes three things to make a marriage: leaving one's parents, cleaving to one's wife, and sexual union.

No one or two of them make a marriage. Leaving home and having sex is not marriage. Nor is leaving home and cleaving to one's wife. Nor is cleaving (if it were possible) without leaving home. Imagine a young man saying to his bride,
"Well, we've had the marriage service. We're going to be true to each other. But now we'll both go back to our homes again, and see each other every Saturday."

Or a girl saying, "We'll leave home, have a wedding and commit ourselves to each other, but there'll be no sex."

Or the most common, "We'll set up house and have sex, but there's no need for a commitment."

You see, none of these plans are any good. All three

aspects must be present for a valid and workable marriage.

Matthew tells us that Jesus once quoted these words from Genesis about marriage. But he added something very significant. This is what He said:
> "What therefore God has joined together, let no man put asunder."
> (Matthew 19:6)

Don't you agree?

## 10. No Trespassing

I have just been at great pains to make the point that it takes more than sex to make a marriage. This is true. In fact, even where for reasons for health or separation no sexual intercourse is possible for a time, a marriage may still stand.

Nevertheless, this is not to say that sex is unimportant—it is very important—very important indeed.

**(1) No trespassing**

Consider the various ways in which you can share with your partner. Most of these areas of sharing are also possible with other people. You can pray, worship, play sports, eat, sing, vacation or work with many different people. In fact, it is virtually impossible to avoid doing these things with many people other than your spouse.

There is really only one area of your marriage that can be kept totally unique and exclusive, and that is the area of sex. This is the one act of sharing that can be restricted between you and your partner alone. This is another reason why even though you may intend to be married, it is still wise to wait until you really are—just to be sure.

If, on the other hand, you engaged in sexual encounters with a number of people, you have nothing left to share exclusively with your husband or wife. The one unique quality of your marriage is sabotaged.

There was a second century Christian who once wrote a letter to a man named Diognetus. In the letter, he attempted to explain what Christianity was all about. In one place, he wrote:
"Any Christian is free to share his neighbor's table, but never his marriage bed."
(Epistle to Diognetus, 5)

Another early Christian apologist wrote something similar. Tertullian, lawyer and Christan scholar, put it very simply:
"Everything is common with us, except our wives."
(Apology, 39, 11)

You have only one thing to give your husband or wife when you marry that you have never given to anyone else. You can bring to your marriage only one unique offering.

Don't spoil it by making it a secondhand gift.

## (2) Take it or give it

Too often, young men in particular seem to think that sex is their natural right. They take girls out in complete confidence that the night will end with sexual intercourse.

Apart from the bad manners behind all this (the assumption that you should be paid for taking the girl out), there is a total misunderstanding of what sex is all about. God-created sexual union is a "giving" relationship—not a "taking" one.

In our story, it says that Amnon "loved" Tamar. Amnon was in love, all right. But it was not with Tamar. He was in love with himself.

All that Amnon wanted was the gratification of his own desire. He wanted to take all, and to give nothing.

But what is love?

That's a question that can't be answered in five minutes. However, we can say this. The essence of it is unselfishness. And this is expressed by giving.

One who truly loves is one who generously gives.

Probably the best-known verse in the Bible is John 3:16. You will remember that it begins, "For God so loved...that he gave..." Love always expresses itself in giving. To selfishly seek sexual gratification without aiming at giving is not love. It is lust.

Sexual intercourse, then, is an expression of giving. Its aim is to give pleasure to the other person. That it gives pleasure to the giver at the same time is evidence of the goodness of God. If it were not so, it would be an intolerable act, offensive to both parties.

When you think about it, all necessary functions are associated with pleasure. Eating is a necessity, but how delightful that it should also be a pleasure! Sleep is a necessity, but isn't it good that it is also a pleasure. So also with drinking, exercise, and so on. So also with sex.

But just as people can eat, or drink, only for the pleasure, and not for the necessity, so it is possible to indulge in sex only for the pleasure. And this, of course, often happens.

I once wrote a few lines in which I referred to:
 "Taking-giving, seeking-finding love."
Love is like that: it works both ways. But it is only really successful when its motive is primarily the pleasure and well-being of the other person.

I know of one young man who thought that when he was married his wife would reach a climax as easily as he did—more or less automatically. So, for a long time, their marriage was marked by clumsy attempts at intercourse in which he was satisfied regularly but in which his wife was not.

Eventually, he learned that she would not automatically respond at the same time as he. In fact, it was his duty to make sure that she was brought to orgasm before he allowed himself to reach a climax. He had to act unselfishly, in other words, expressing real love by aiming first at giving her pleasure, and only then thinking of himself. His bride, on the other hand, also had to see that she did not cause him to wait too long too often—for she had to concentrate on giving him pleasure, too.

When two people work together at pleasing one another, then sex is fulfilling its proper role.

As I have mentioned, relaxed pleasure is really only possible within the security and warmth of marriage. Any who try to snatch selfishly at their own pleasure are not only wrong, but also stupid: for the end result will be disappointment for both.

### (3) If music be the food of love, play on

I suppose that nearly all the great music of the world has been written either about love of a man for his God, or of a man for a woman—or vice versa.

Music is very often associated with love.

One of the characters in Shakespeare's *Twelfth Night* calls music the "food of love." And no wonder. For music and love are very similar. The longer you practice the more beautiful it becomes.

And this is another reason why a sexual relationship needs the right kind of environment to develop fully. This may be a startling revelation to some of the young people who read this book, but it is nevertheless true, that the pleasure of sex actually improves as the years go by.

Your parents probably enjoy their sex life more now than they did when they were your age. To young people who simply cannot imagine anyone over twenty-five even making love, this may sound surprising. But I assure you it is true—in those cases, of course, where the right principles are applied. (Some parents still have not learned the basic lessons of marriage relationships and so they still battle with tension and dissatisfaction. But it need not be so.)

Furthermore, Christian couples can have a more fulfilling and satisfying relationship than non-Christians. This may also seem startling, especially to those who regard Christians as narrow-minded, strait-laced, sour people. But remember that Jesus Christ described the Christian life as an abundant life (John 10:10). This includes sex! If you want the best kind of sex relationship in your marriage, commit it to Christ and build it on Christian principles.

It's something like this. A bride and a bridegroom are like two people learning to play musical instruments together. Take a harp and a violin, for instance. Played incorrectly, both of them can be

distressing, especially the violin. But played together well, they can make beautiful music.

In marriage, the instruments are the human bodies themselves. Each member of the partnership learns how to bring out beautiful harmony from the other. Together, they play fine music. Each must regard the other highly. Expensive instruments cannot be treated harshly. A delicate touch is far more likely to produce beauty than a harsh one.

Too many men treat their wives like drums to be beaten, or electric guitars to be played hard and fast: the instrument is left quivering and pounded, or even worse, silent and musically dead.

Two people who are prepared to learn to make music together can reach heights of delight that would otherwise be left unrealized.

### (4) The two shall become three

One of the biggest dangers with illicit sex is the possibility of childbirth. Even though they are not 100 percent safe, the ready availability of contraceptives these days has reduced this risk to some extent. (Not that I am advocating this, of course!)

Now, it's the innocent girls that usually get caught. The promiscuous ones take precautions. Those who don't intend to have intercourse, but do so in the heat of the moment, are often the ones who become pregnant.

What if pregnancy does result from premarital sex? What can you do? There are several alternatives that can be followed—but none of them are good ones.

A hasty marriage can be arranged, for example. But hasty marriages are often unsuccessful. I can think of several couples who married on this basis alone and whose marriages have failed.

Another alternative is for the mother to keep the child and bring it up herself, alone. This is commonly done these days. However, children need the love, care, protection and completeness that mother and father together provide. If, through death, a child is deprived of a father, then both mother and child must make the best of it—clearly this is beyond their control. But if a girl deliberately chooses to "go it alone" she could be making a risky decision.

A third line of action, which is gaining in popularity with frightening speed, is abortion.

In the United States, alone, there is now at least one abortion to every four live births!

But the most important thing for us to look at is what the Scriptures say about the unborn child growing within a mother's womb. The Psalmist, David, reveals God's firsthand involvement in the

creation of a new human life:
> "For thou didst form my inward parts, thou didst knit me together in my mother's womb." (Psalm 139:13)

And in the book of Jeremiah the Lord Himself declares His place in that creation:
> "Now the word of the Lord came to me saying, 'Before I formed you in the womb I knew you, And before you were born I consecrated you, And I appointed you a prophet to the nations.'" (Jeremiah 1:5)

God not only *forms* a new human being in the womb, He knows all about that child *even before conception takes place!* We must be careful not to violate the life that God Himself has created.

I am sure that most girls who contemplate abortion do not understand the actual abilities of the child within them even at the earliest stages of development.

At three weeks the tiny human being is only one-tenth of an inch long, but already has the beginnings of a spinal cord, nervous system, eyes, lungs, stomach and intestines. And the tiny heart has begun beating even before this, at the 18th day. By six-and-a-half weeks, the baby has begun to move, a full three months before the mother might even feel the first "kick."

At eight weeks the developing child can do many

things: suck his thumb, get hiccups, make a fist, wake and sleep. At sixteen weeks he already has formed toes, fingers and facial features. Finally, at eighteen weeks this tiny human being becomes large and active enough for his mother to feel the movements as he punches and kicks, flexing his developing muscles. This is what is often referred to as "quickening." But long before this, when many women might be having an abortion, a tiny growing human being is alive within the womb.

The long-term effects of guilt from having an abortion have yet to be discovered. However, experiencing anywhere from mild to extremely severe guilt feelings over ending a young life is a very real possibility, even for the fathers involved.

Once, after a meeting where I had spoken on abortion, a man approached me and said, "What you say about abortion and guilt is absolutely right. I know from experience."

"What do you mean?" I asked him.

"About five years ago, my wife become pregnant," he answered. "We couldn't face having another baby then, so we decided on an abortion."

"Why?"

"That's the terrible part. There was no real reason at all. I suppose we felt we couldn't afford it, it would be inconvenient and so on."

"So?"

"Well," he continued, "we discovered that we didn't have to have a reason. It was no trouble at all to arrange for the pregnancy to be terminated. But after it was done, I experienced great guilt. I wasn't outwardly depressed, but I was so inwardly disturbed that I seriously contemplated suicide!

"It was then that the Lord met me and saved me. Both my wife and I became Christians and the guilt has now been dealt with. It's no longer a problem, praise God.

"But I don't know what would have happened if we had not come to Christ."

This incident—describing a *father's* feelings—is very revealing, isn't it?

So, as a final word of caution to those who have come to believe that abortion is modern medicine's "easy way out"—think twice and count the cost of your decision!

The fourth alternative for an unwanted pregnancy is adoption. In this case, the child is at least given a chance to be brought up in a happy, secure, loving environment. And childless parents are given the opportunity of raising children in their own home.

But here again, there is often suffering. I can think of one girl who decided on adoption as her only course of action. But even now, three or four years later, she still finds it hard to handle, particularly when she is in the presence of children about the age of her child. And there are countless records of adopted children who later suffer emotionally with a feeling of rejection from their real parents.

There is, however, one way to avoid the anguish of *any* of these decisions. It is simple: save sex for marriage! Thus, God's true intention is fullfilled, and the abundant joy that giving birth to children provides can be fully realized.

You see, the best environment for the baby is still the family. It was ordained by God and has never been bettered. Before two people claim the right to intercourse, then, they should set up the kind of relationship where the fruits of intercourse— children—can be properly nurtured.

Actually, it is irresponsible to expect to have sexual relationships without, at the same time, being prepared to have a family. God's pattern seems to be: family or celibacy.

But the point I really want to make here is this: One of the fundamental purposes of sex is child-rearing. It is one of the most joyful, satisfying experiences two people can ever share.

Years ago, the song writer David wrote:
"Lo, the sons are a heritage from the Lord,
   the fruit of the womb a reward.

> Like arrows in the hand of a warrior
> are the sons of one's youth.
> Happy is the man who has his quiver full of them!"
> (Psalm 127:3-5)

Children are a gift from God. They bring into the home a spirit of joy, unselfishness, and sharing that nothing else can produce. Happy indeed is the man who is a father.

And what a marvelous thing to know that the very means by which you uniquely and exclusively express your love for your partner is the same means by which you produce children who are uniquely and exclusively yours.

Don't settle for a marriage arrangement which makes childbirth impossible. If you do, you are again settling for less than the best. (Of course, I am not referring to people who are *unable* to bear children—that is a different matter.)

**(5) The first shall be last**

Have you ever realized that the first time in your life that you have intercourse is also the last time it can ever be the first time?

There is only one first time!

Why not share it with the right person?

Even if that first attempt is not very successful or very satisfying, you can still look back on it with nostalgia, or fun, or amusement, for it was something that the two of you shared together exclusively.

If you have already experienced the first time, but with the wrong person, we must honestly say that you have done something that can never be reversed. Nevertheless, if you commit yourself to the Lord Jesus Christ, your past can be forgiven and cleansed. So when you do marry, because your past has been cleansed, it will almost be the same as the first time ever. And of course it *will* be the first time with the person that God has chosen for you, which is still a blessing to remember.

### (6) V.D. 1977

I am writing this in the year A.D. 1977. Anno Domini: In the year of the Lord.

For thousands of young people, however, it is the year V.D. 1977. For in spite of our sophistication, our medical advances and our scientific knowledge, veneral disease is still rampant, and in more places than it has ever been.

As you can see from these statistics, despite the availability of modern antibiotics, venereal disease is certainly on the increase! The number of cases of gonorrhea reported in the United States has increased over 60 percent between 1971 and

## Recent U.S. Figures

| Year | Gonorrhea | Infectious Syphilis |
|------|-----------|---------------------|
| 1971 | 624,371   | 41,179              |
| 1972 | 718,401   | 44,354              |
| 1973 | 809,681   | 47,973              |
| 1974 | 874,161   | 49,018              |
| 1975 | 938,778   | 51,912              |
| 1976 | 1,007,518 | 51,037              |

1976; while infectious syphilis has been almost steadily on the rise also. (And these figures only apply to those cases *reported*. Because of the nature of the disease, it is often kept secret.) Those cases which are not reported or treated early enough can result in grave physical and mental impairment and even death.

Furthermore, these statistics don't reveal the disastrous results to babies born of infected mothers. Often these children are blind from birth, mentally retarded, or have numerous birth defects, as well as the venereal disease itself!

Need I say more?

It's not good enough to laugh away the threat of V.D. as "old-fashioned," or "prudish," or "alarmist." It is still a dangerous and *deadly* complaint.

Venereal disease is most commonly passed on through sexual intercourse. If you play around with sex, you run a very real danger of suffering from it. On the other hand, if you remain faithful to one partner within the safety of marriage, you are unlikely to even get near it.

Is it worth the risk?

## (7) But I like it

If I haven't convinced you yet that premarital sex is an act of folly, then it can be for only one reason. You're doing it and you like it.

And that is the most difficult of all objections to overcome with any sin. Until you are prepared to dislike it, you'll never stop. In fact, Jesus took it even further. He said that any man who "does not hate...even his own life, cannot be my disciple" (Luke 14:26).

You say, "But how can I hate it if I like it?"

Only God can help you to do that. He will show you what sin really is. You will realize that it was sin that put Jesus Christ on the cross. You will see that the pleasure that you enjoy was deep pain for Him. You will understand that sin is so bad that it cost the life of the Lord Jesus Christ to atone for it.

Why not talk to the Lord about it and ask Him to show you how things really stand?

And remember the words that we have already

read from that great, lovable disciple of Christ, Simon Peter:

> "His divine power has granted to us *all things* that pertain to life and godliness, through the *knowledge of him* who called us to his own glory and excellence, by which he has granted to us his precious and very great promises, that *through these* you may *escape* the corruption that is in the world because of passion, and become partakers of the divine nature."

You see, it *is* possible to escape the corruption of passion. By *knowing* Jesus, we *can* share His own excellence. Victory over sin *is* yours, if you want it.

What pleasure you may now be experiencing in illicit sex is only a poor imitation of the real pleasure that a properly fulfilled sexual relationship offers. Furthermore, there is an exhilaration, an exultant joy in living in victory over sin according to the promises of God. Couple the joy of holiness with the joy of loving someone according to God's holy Word, and you're really living!

Don't settle for anything less!

## 11. Till Death Do Us Part

*"Then Amnon hated her with a very great hatred; so that the hatred with which he hated her was greater than the love with which he had loved her."*

The ironic thing about lust is that it destroys itself.

It cannot rest until it gains what it longs for—but in the very gaining it dies. The tragedy of Tamar was in this very thing. Amnon, who claimed to love her most passionately, now hated her with even greater passion.

So he had his servant put her out and drive her away. And all he can call her now is "this woman."

Tamar's story is the story of a thousand other girls who lost their virginity in the same way. To give it to a man who will protect you and stand by you in marriage is no loss at all. But to lose it to a man who now despises you for it is a desperate wrong. Many a girl has yielded to the passionate demands of her lover, in the hope of keeping him by doing so. But in the very yielding she has lost him.

Girls! Guard yourselves jealously. Your body is the temple of the Holy Spirit given to you by God. Don't abandon it to the selfish, passing lust of a passionate boy who is too weak to control himself.

Fellows! Why should it always be the girl who is expected to say "No"? Yet this is the approach most young men adopt.

"I'll go as far as she'll let me," they think. And if she doesn't prevent it, they will simply keep on going. Wouldn't it be better for a fellow to set his own limits and keep to them?

I had a young couple come to me once who solved the problem *together*. They were disarmingly frank in their conversations with each other, and with my wife and me.

"Well, how are things going?" I asked.

"Terrific," said Andy.

"Any problems?"

"We did have," answered Cathy. "But we think we're working them out."

"Go on," I answered.

"Well, our main difficulty was when we got by ourselves," Andy confessed. "We found ourselves going further than we really intended to." I must have looked worried, for he quickly added, "But not all the way!"

He continued. "But we could see red lights flashing. So we both agreed on how far we should go and where we should stop."

"What did you decide?"

"In simple terms, that we would kiss and embrace, but that we'd keep all our clothes on! And no hands underneath, either."

They'd obviously had a very frank discussion.

But this is the sort of thing young people who are in love need to do. Set limits and keep to them. Don't go too close to the cliff edge. Then you're in no danger of going over.

I gave these two the further advice of staying where they could be interrupted, which they happily accepted.

They are now married and doing very well.

Here, however, was one young man who was prepared to take a stand, establish a limit and keep to it. Even though he was engaged to the girl he would not take advantage of her. Nor would he run the risk of afterwards discarding her.

But back to our original story.

Amnon ultimately had his problems, too.

You may remember that Tamar had a brother named Absalom. Absalom knew all that had happened between his little sister and Amnon, and he was determined to do something about it. But he bided his time.

It was not, in fact, until "two full years" later that he acted. Absalom organized a feast and invited Amnon. The scheme was more subtle than Amnon's own scheme to ensnare Tamar—but just as deceitful.

At the feast, when Amnon had been drinking till "his heart was merry with wine," Absalom commanded his servants to rise up and slay him. And this they did.

Now I am not going to say that if you rape a girl you will be knocked off two years later. In fact, there are numerous adulterers and fornicators walking our streets today.

But I *am* prepared to say that in some way your sin will catch up with you. A long time ago, Moses, leader of God's people, warned the tribe of Reuben to fulfill their duties. "But if you will not do so," he continued, "behold, you have sinned against the

Lord; and be sure your sin will find you out" (Numbers 32:23).

Now look at this carefully. It doesn't say that your sin will be *found* out—but that it will *find you* out. In other words, sooner or later, whether your sin is discovered or not, it will affect you in some way. Sooner or later, the poison of sin achieves its deadly purpose.

You can't play with sin and get away with it.

Your only safeguard is to avoid sin and thus be sure. And, of course, there is the good news that if you have sinned, you can be forgiven through Jesus Christ. Then you can make a new start.

A couple of years ago, I spoke to a youth group on the story of Amnon and Tamar.

At the conclusion of the service, I invited young people who wanted to commit themselves to God, or to put right some past failure, or to seek strength for the future, to move to an adjoining prayer room where they could pray and find an answer in Jesus Christ.

I did not know it until afterwards, but there were three young people present who had been almost reenacting the very story.

First, there was a "Tamar." Secondly, there was an "Absalom." He was not "Tamar's" brother, but he did feel a brotherly concern for her, and a desire to protect her.

Then there was an "Amnon." He was a fellow who had played fast and loose with the girls, and had done just this with "Tamar." He had courted her, and seduced her, and discarded her.

She was obviously still drawn to him. Like Tamar of old, she knew that this "Amnon" had done wrong in seducing her, but felt that he had done *a greater wrong in discarding her*. She was obviously trying to regain his affection.

Meanwhile, her "Absalom" had found out what had happened. And he was deeply bitter against "Amnon."

So there they all were.

A "Tamar" who was fruitlessly hoping to regain the affection of the boy who had seduced her.

An "Amnon" who having had his fun didn't seem to care any more about the girl.

And an "Absalom" whose bitterness kept him from fellowship with "Amnon."

It was an explosive situation. Fortunately, this modern "Absalom" had no intention of taking his enemy's life. But he hated him, which, in terms of the Sermon on the Mount, amounted to the same thing.

Then came the challenge at the end of the service. The two young men were among the first who went to the prayer room. There a great deal of heart-searching was done. The results were drastic.

"Amnon" was not seen at church again for weeks. He had faced up to his behavior, it seemed, and felt ashamed. But finally, he did return and, as far as I know, is living an upright life now.

"Absalom" committed himself and his hatred to Christ. He came out of the prayer room a changed person. I believe he told his parents that he felt God calling him to the ministry. Certainly, he had learned to forgive.

I don't know what happened to "Tamar." She didn't seem to be helped by the service. I do not know where she is now.

I hope that she, too, has found a new life. But if she hasn't, she is the tragic victim of an unscrupulous young man—just as the original Tamar was.

This chapter is headed "Till death do us part." In the case of Amnon and Tamar, the death of their relationship came almost as soon as it began: it was stillborn. And Amnon's own death came much sooner than he expected.

It need not be so. When a relationship is properly

founded, and given time to develop and grow, it should last for years. The phrase "till death do us part" is meant to convey the idea of a lifelong partnership—an enduring relationship. This is what it ought to be.

Why not let it be so with you?

# **TAMAR REMEMBERS**

(2 Samuel 13:12-14)


They used to envy me, the other girls;
My beauty and the glances it provoked
From Amnon and his bragging fellow-churls
Were seen by them as charms to be invoked!
Would God that He had blasted me with pox
Or scars or ugliness or leprosy!
It could not have been worse than comeliness.
Now desolate and crushed with memory
Of shame and restless, helpless bitterness,
I yearn to live again that aching, pointless day,
To change the lines, to redirect the play,
To batter down the door, break through the locks
That keep me from the past, in misery.

"Forget it now," says Absalom. "He got
What he deserved. It's time to live again!"
But Amnon's death cannot retie the knot—
The cord is cut, my future preordained.
I have been used.

Some years ago, when songs
Danced from his lips, my father wrote these lines:
"Create in me the heart for which my spirit longs,
O God, who washes, cleanses and refines
The sin-scarred soul." If only God would do
The miracle I need and make me new!

## 12. Getting It All Together

There are probably two kinds of young people reading this book (I don't just mean fellows and girls!).

Firstly, there are those who have not sinned sexually, and who want to know how to remain clean. Secondly, there are those who have sinned, and want to know how to become clean as well as how to remain clean.

Let's take the second group first.

If you have committed fornication, the first thing you must do is admit it. Face up to it as sin, repent of it and confess it to God. The Bible says:
"If we confess our sins, he (God) is faithful and just, and will forgive our sins and cleanse us from all unrighteousness."
(1 John 1:9)

Secondly, you must believe that when you have done this, your sins *are* forgiven. You become a

new person. Another passage says:
> "Therefore, if anyone is in Christ, he is a new creation; the old has passed away, behold, the new has come."
> (2 Corinthians 5:17)

Thirdly, you should be baptized as an act of commitment to your new life. Again, the Scripture says:
> "We were buried therefore with him by baptism into death, so that as Christ was raised from the dead by the glory of the Father, we too might walk in newness of life."
> (Romans 6:4)

By baptism you share the death and life of Jesus: your new life in Him becomes a reality.

There are many other things you can do, also. There is daily Bible reading and prayer, and regular fellowship with other Christians in a local church. And so on. You should experience all of these to ensure that your new life is healthy and strong in the Lord.

But I want to come now to the second question: not how to *become* clean, but how to *remain* clean. And I want to relate this particularly to the sexual realm.

In order not to become bogged down in unnecessary detail, I am only going to say three things. They are easy to remember. I hope you will take hold of them.

## The Mind

First of all, *guard your mind!* Don't let your mind be like a rubbish bin with the lid off, where people can drop whatever they like. Let it be a food cabinet, into which only wholesome food is placed.

Now this is entirely up to you. What goes into your thought life is what you allow to go in. If you read suggestive books, view degrading films, and let your mind wander through lurid by-paths, then you cannot help but stir up your sexual desires.

One young friend of mine, Peter, was a Christian art student. One day he happened to mention to me that he had been to an R-film.

"What were you doing there?" I asked.

"I wanted to see it because of the spectacular photography in it," he replied.

"But what about the rest of it?" I continued. "How can you sit through that kind of stuff without being disturbed?"

"It doesn't worry me, Pastor. I see worse things than that every day at the art school. R-films just don't worry me in the slightest."

I glanced at my wife, who was making coffee. I saw

that she, too, was mildly amused by Peter's arrogance.

"I don't believe you," I said, deliberately.

"No, it's true. They really don't worry me at all. I can just enjoy the photography and ignore the rest."

The conversation drifted on to other things.

A few months later, Peter fell in love with a sweet Christian girl—a bright, cheerful lass who was just what he needed. She taught him humility, for a start! But the fact is that they were head over heels in love. (They're now married and still buoyantly happy.)

And suddenly his standards changed. Now that he was experiencing real love for the first time, he saw through the cheap eroticism, the shallow sexuality of the theater. He realized that in spite of his open-mindedness—in fact, because of it—his own standards were being cheapened.

One night, Peter and his fiancée went to see a comedy that my wife and I had seen and very much enjoyed. We thought (and still think) that it was a good, clean, funny film. But Peter came home enraged.

"The whole thing was stupid and degrading!" he declared. "And what about that engagement that broke up! What was funny about that?"

Actually, it was a case of "better to break the engagement than to enter a disastrous marriage." But Peter's concepts had reversed so much that he was now more stringent than we were! It took genuine affection for a girl to make him realize how cheap and degrading much of the world's entertainment is.

It's a pity that his love for Christ hadn't taught him the same thing first.

You can't fill your thoughts with rubbish and not be affected.

Let me repeat it. What your mind feeds on is up to you. You can choose the books you read, the films you see, the places you go, the songs you sing.

You can bring every thought captive to obey Christ.

**The Spirit**

Being a Christian is not just turning over a new leaf. It is more than "living a decent life."

Being a Christian is *experiencing a spiritual union with Christ*. I have already quoted the verse that says,
 "He who is united with the Lord becomes one
 spirit with him."
 (1 Corinthians 6:17)

You enter a new dimension of living. You are indeed a new person.

In addition to this, you now have power at your disposal to overcome sin—it is now possible for you to live a victorious life.

Let's look again at the verse from Peter that has already been quoted a couple of times:
> "His divine power *has granted to us all things* that pertain to life and godliness..."

In other words, you have everything at your fingertips that you need to overcome temptation and live rightly.

Isn't this wonderful? It means that it is always possible to be clean. But what it also means is that there is never any reason for sinning! (And that's not so exciting because it leaves us without excuse!)

In simple terms: YOU DON'T HAVE TO SIN.

Can you get hold of that? You don't *have* to sin. You can be victorious over sin. Temptation is not too strong for you. The devil is not too powerful for you. The feelings you have when your sweetheart is in your arms are not uncontrollable.

You are a human being, a child of God, a son or daughter of the King, a conqueror of Satan, a new creation in Christ Jesus! Who is there who can overcome you? What temptation is there which can master you?

Be strong in the Lord and in the power of His might!

This concept that I am sharing with you now has meant a lot to me personally. There have been times in my own life when I have tried to rationalise sin. I have tried to convince myself that "in this case it's all right. There are certain exceptional circumstances which throw a different light on things."

But I have found safety in reaffirming these truths!

—I don't have to sin.

—There is never any excuse for sin.

—I can be free from sin through the power of Jesus Christ.

And I remember the joy with which my own congregation received a message that I preached one morning on a text from the book of Deuteronomy. It says:
> "For this commandment which I command you this day *is not too hard for you,* neither is it far off...
> But the word is very near you; it is in your mouth and in your heart, so that you *can* do it."
> (Deuteronomy 30:11-14)

In other words, whatever commands God gives are also promises. What God *asks* us to do, he *enables* us to do.

His commandment is not too hard: you *can* do it!

**The Body**

"All of which is very good," you may say. "But what do I do about the desires that I feel in my body whether I ask for them or not?"

This is a real problem, I must agree.

Even if you do control your thought life, and try to believe God, you may still be under pressure from desires that arise naturally, particularly if you are a fellow.

There is nothing wrong with such desires, of course. They are natural and universal. But it must be stated again, that they are also controllable. You don't have to give in to them.

"That's okay for you," you may say, "you're married. You can satisfy your sexual urges whenever you like."

Can I?

In fact, this is not true. Marriage is not an open go to satisfy sexual urge. I think this has probably been made plain already in this book. On an average, most married couples probably engage in sexual intercourse two or three times a week. Some do so more frequently, some less. It depends on the couple themselves, the kind of work they are doing, the hours they keep, and so on. It's not just "open go." But let me take it a little further. What happens within marriage?

Often, the answer is tiredness, sickness, busyness, pregnancies, and sometimes separations. In all of these cases, there is some time of enforced abstinence from intercourse—and the necessary self-control.

In my own case, sickness rarely troubles us as God keeps my whole family in good health. But we have three children, and even though my wife had wonderfully healthy pregnancies, she was still unable to enjoy intercourse during the latter months and the first few months after childbirth.

Secondly, I am often away from home on ministry tours for periods of days or weeks at a time. I don't enjoy these separations very much. But I do have opportunity to practice the self-control that I enjoin on others!

Even within marriage, then, there is often the need for personal integrity and victory in the sexual realm.

There is one practical way which may be of help to some young people. I am careful in sharing this, for it is not a magic cure-all, a gimmick to avoid personal faith and trust in God's promises. But in the context of those promises it can aid in self-discipline. I'm referring to fasting.

To set aside a day, or two or three days, for prayer and fasting enables you to concentrate solely on the Word of God and the promises it contains. It also allows your body to experience abstinence from food, and helps you to practice mastery of physical desires. And in practical terms, it probably does you good physically, anyway.

Teenage years are not easy. But they *are* exciting. There are a thousand things to learn and experience. Tread carefully and joyfully in Christ and you can enjoy them to the full.

Let me finish this first part of the book with a story.

Sharon is now a bride of many years. She has a fine husband and is very happy. Before she committed her life to Christ, she had several sexual encounters with fellows for whom she felt nothing.

Some months after her wedding, my wife and I were talking with her about marriage and offering such advice as was necessary.

I asked her a direct question.

"Sharon, do you mind if I ask you a personal

question? If you don't want to answer it you don't have to."

"What is it?"

"Well, can you tell us how you would compare your sexual relationship now with the experiences you had years ago? Is there much difference?"

I really knew what her answer would be, but I wasn't quite prepared for the reaction I got.

She looked at me as if there was something wrong with me. You would think I had asked her if she knew the sum of two and two. I could imagine her thinking, "What a ridiculous question."

But then she smiled, sheepishly, but proudly, and simply said, "There just isn't any comparison—it's so completely different."

What made the difference?

Love? Marriage? God? Her husband?

All of these things. But I think the complete answer is *commitment*. This time, her sexual relationship was part of a total relationship. Because she and her husband were committed, they could relax with each other and fully enjoy one another.

Of course, there was love. There was God. They

were Christians. Those things are all *part* of commitment.

But essentially, Sharon enjoyed her love because it was *secure* in both her husband and in Jesus Christ.

If you settle for anything less, you yourself will be the loser.

# PART TWO

## 13. The Purpose of Sex

So many people have a distorted idea of what the Bible really does teach about sex that it is necessary to state it here in clear and simple terms.

Much of this has been referred to indirectly in the course of this book. Here, it is summarized in a concise, systematic fashion. Naturally, all of these points are seen as being fulfilled in the context of marriage *only*.

### (1) Gratification

The Scriptures freely admit that sexual intercourse provides an outlet for the gratification of physical desire. This is what Paul says:
> "Because of the temptation to immorality, each man should have his own wife, and each woman her own husband. The husband should give to his wife her conjugal (i.e. sexual) rights, and likewise the wife to her husband...It is better to marry than to be aflame with passion." (1 Corinthians 7:2, 3, 9)

Now that is very clear. Paul openly faces the fact that most people experience desire for sexual fulfillment, and he advocates marriage as a cure for this. And within marriage, each partner must freely give gratification to the other, as far as this is possible.

It is remarkable that so many people accuse Paul of being antisex, antifeminist, and antimarriage. It is true that he did suggest that for those who would serve the Lord actively, the single life may be advantageous. But apart from this, he clearly teaches marriage as a normal, healthy state.

So, a valid purpose of sex in marriage is simply the gratification of desire.

## (2) Procreation

Procreation is a word that means literally "creation on behalf of." In this case, it is an act of creation on behalf of God. Thus, it refers to childbirth.

Obviously, one of the purposes of sexual relations is procreation. Right in the beginning, God said to the people He Himself created:
"Be fruitful and multiply, and fill the earth and subdue it..."
(Genesis 1:28)

This is one reason why expecting to have sex without ever intending to have children is wrong.

It is like wanting only dessert without any vegetables. It is selling yourself short.

In the second century, Justin Martyr wrote that Christians of his day had sexual intercourse only when they wanted to have children. This was, as we have seen, a departure from God's plan and purpose. Sex is far more comprehensive than this. However, procreation is still an important purpose. It cannot be ignored.

Like eating vegetables, raising children has its moments of unpleasantness, but in the long run it is satisfying and enjoyable. In fact, people who want sex without procreation do not know how much they are depriving themselves of deep pleasure and joy.

Remember the psalmist said:
"Lo, sons are a heritage from the Lord,
 the fruit of the womb a reward...
Happy is the man who has his quiver full of them..."
(Psalm 127:3, 5)

### (3) Recreation

A very important function for sex is recreation. It is a delightful means by which a husband and wife can simply enjoy being with each other. It is a means of recreation and pleasure which they can share together uniquely. They may play bridge or tennis with the neighbors; but their sexual games are theirs alone.

There is a fascinating little incident in the life of the Old Testament patriarch, Isaac, which illustrates this.

When he and his wife, Rebekah, were dwelling in the land of Gerar, Isaac feared that because of Rebekah the local men might kill him to marry her. So he let it be known that Rebekah was only his sister. If they thought she was his sister, his life would no longer be in danger. It was a silly scheme, of course, as well as deceitful, and it deserved to fail.

One day, Isaac and Rebekah met in a garden, where they thought they were alone. Unknown to them, the king of Gerar, Abimelech, saw them through a window.

And the story says:
 "Abimelech, king of the Philistines looked out of a window and saw Isaac fondling Rebekah his wife.
 So Abimelech called Isaac, and said, 'Behold, she is your wife...'"
 (Genesis 26:8-9)

The King James Bible says that Isaac was "sporting" with Rebekah. The Living Bible translates the word as "petting." The root of the original Hebrew word means literally to "laugh" or "play."

Put all this together and we have a delightful picture of Isaac and Rebekah enjoying love-play together. They weren't just playing ring-a-rosie. They were playing the kind of game that made it obvious they were husband and wife!

Sex is for recreation! It's good fun.

This is also brought out very clearly in the Song of Solomon. Many people read the book as a parable of the relationship between Christ and His church. It is this. But it is first of all a series of very exciting and very frank love songs. And if you read the book right through, you will sense a spirit of joy and delight in the relationship between the bride and her groom.

In the Book of Proverbs there is another interesting passage. It says:
"Rejoice in the wife of your youth...
Let her affection fill you at all times with delight, be infatuated always with her love."
(Proverbs 5: 18-19)
The word here rendered "affection" is literally "breasts" (as in the King James Bible). So here is another frank and honest statement from the Bible about sex. A woman's breasts are attractive to a man. So, let both parties realize this, and let a wife's breasts fill her husband with delight!

There is *real joy* to be experienced in a Biblical sex relationship!

Furthermore, the primary meaning of the word "recreation" is "creating again." True recreation rebuilds strength and courage for the resumption of work. Sexual recreation is like this. It refreshes, it stimulates, it encourages, it strengthens, it enlivens. Happy lovers walk with a spring in their step and a joy in their eyes.

These are not just features of falling in love. They are results of remaining in love. Sex, properly enjoyed, is truly recreative.

## (4) Communication

*The most vital purpose of sex is communication.* The word communication, however, must be understood in its fullest sense. It's not just sending a letter or making a telephone call. It is based on the word "commune" which implies spending time with another person and really getting to know them.

This is why in some places in the Bible the word "know" is used with the meaning "have intercourse with." Cain was born to Adam and Eve, for example, because Adam "knew" his wife (Genesis 4:1). Before her marriage, Rebekah was a virgin "whom no man had known" (Genesis 24:16). Jesus was born to Mary, although Joseph "knew her not" (Matthew 1:25).

The word "know" is clearly used in a special sense here. There is a kind of knowledge in sexual intercourse that is quite unique. Again, this is the one area of a marriage that can be totally exclusive. You can know other people in many different ways—indeed, you can't avoid doing so. But there is one kind of knowledge that you can keep just between the two of you: you can make it entirely yours—and that is your sexual knowledge of each other.

The essence of communication is sharing. In its simplest form it means to share news with someone else. In its fullest form it means giving all that you have and are to another. It is used in this way in the Bible. And that is what sex is really all about. You can give to each other a special kind of pleasure that nothing else can give. Indeed, you give yourselves to each other totally, with nothing between. There is no cover-up, no deception.

Sex which does not have such personal, intimate knowledge as its ultimate aim is very much less than the kind of sex the Bible talks about.

In other words, sex is not just the sharing of two bodies. It is an expression of the sharing of two personalities: spirit, mind *and* body. Christian people may intersperse love-making with talking, playing, praying, sharing in any genuine way. For it is in this way that true knowledge of one another is achieved.

And this is another reason why sexual intercourse is the end of courting, not the beginning of it. It is the climax of getting to know each other, not the start.

And over the years, it is a continuing expression of an ever-deepening mutual knowledge.

## (5) Love

It may seem surprising that love is the last thing in this list. Gratification, procreation, recreation, and communication may seem to be far less noble things than love.

But actually, love includes these things. None of the others make sense without it. For love is more than just butterflies in the stomach and occasional skipped heartbeats. Love is essentially giving. And it is only when people learn to give to each other that they can find total fulfillment in sexual relationships.

Gratification or recreation or even communication without love are empty things. So the bride in the Song of Solomon sighs:
 "Upon my bed at night I sought him whom my *soul* loves..."
 (Song of Solomon 3:1)
This is a deeper thing than a physical relationship. There is in her heart a soul-longing of which her physical longing is but an expression.

I have deliberately left love till last in this discussion to make it clear that it is not just a sentimental, romantic thing. It is an act of unselfish commitment to a person with whom you are fully prepared to share your life. It has far less to do with feelings than most people realize.

Feelings may stem from love, but they are not love. Love is a matter of decision—of will. We decide to love because we want to do so.

One Christian writer has said, "Love is an *unconditional* commitment to an *imperfect* person." It means loving one another, just as you are.

It is a matter of giving. We want to give to the object of love, not to take.

It is a matter of knowing. We want to know the object of love above all else.

It is a matter of pleasure. We want to enjoy the sharing of our love.

But whether pleasure is received or not, love may still exist. For love is basic. It is the beginning and end of all lasting relationships. It is the opening of oneself to another. It is the greatest of all human activities. It is distinguished by being equated with the greatest Being known to man. For in three short words, the whole of love may be embraced. You find them in the Bible. It simply says,
 "God is love."

## 14. Celibacy
*Some advantages of the single life*

Quite often, young men and women wonder whether it is God's will for them to remain single or not. They read Paul's wish that all men were as he was and feel mildly disturbed by it.

Let it be clearly stated that marriage is normal for men and women. From the beginning, as we have seen, God ordained that a man "should leave his father and mother and be joined to his wife." But, nevertheless, there may be occasions when celibacy is desirable. Let's see what the Bible says.

Firstly, the Lord Jesus Christ taught that the ability to live a single life is only for those who are able to "receive" it. In a discussion on this subject, He made it plain that not everyone can endure a lifetime of being single. So He concluded:
   "He who is able to receive this, let him receive it."
   (Matthew 19:12)

Paul took this a little further when he wrote:
> "I wish that all were as I myself am. But each has his own special gift from God, one of one kind and one of another."
> (1 Corinthians 7:7)

In other words, some have the gift of being happily married; others have the gift of being happily single. If God wants you to be single, He will see that you are able to handle it joyfully.

Unfortunately, there is often a kind of slur on single people. They are regarded with "compassion," as if there were something wrong with them. Or, they are ignored, and the valuable role that they have both in the world and in the church is overlooked.

In first Corinthians chapter seven, Paul lists four advantages of celibacy. We will take them in order.

### (1) Mastery

The celibate person is one who has achieved a degree of self-mastery not possible for the married. He has learned to totally and permanently control the desires of the flesh. So when Paul says, "If they cannot exercise self-control, they should marry," he is implying that if they can exercise self-control, then it may be better not to marry.

The single person, then, has a unique opportunity for personal mastery that others may not share.

## (2) Peace of mind

Paul saw marriage as a blessing, but as a blessing accompanied by "worldly troubles" (verse 28). So, for him, another motive for being single is to avoid this. So he writes,

> "Those who marry will have worldly troubles, and I would spare you that."

A single man or woman has much less to worry about and far fewer problems to solve. Of course, a married person joyfully accepts these additional responsibilities. But the single Christian may equally joyfully reject them!

## (3) Undivided interests

This is really Paul's main argument in favor of celibacy. It enables a man or woman to give more attention to the things of God. This is what he writes:

> "The unmarried man is anxious about the affairs of the Lord, how to please the Lord; but the married man is anxious about worldly affairs, how to please his wife, and his interests are divided."
>
> (1 Corinthians 7:32-34)

This is not an absolute conflict, of course. Thousands of married men are concerned about the things of God *and* the things of the home. Indeed, the two may be one in some ways.

But nevertheless, it is true that a single person has

far more time and attention for the Lord's work—more time to study, to pray, to attend meetings, to be involved in the community, to serve one's neighbor and so on than a married person.

## (4) Undivided loyalty

This last point naturally follows, of course. If you can devote more time to God's work, then you can show more loyalty. This time Paul says:
"I say this for your own benefit, not to lay any restraint upon you, but to promote good order and to secure your undivided devotion to the Lord."
(1 Corinthians 7:35)
So the single person may be undivided in his loyalties, for there is no conflict.

I have experienced this in a small way myself. I am involved in regular trips away from home to lecture or teach. Most times, this is only for a few days. Sometimes it involves several weeks. Much as I am lonely and miss my wife, I also appreciate the opportunity this gives for spending more time in prayer and waiting upon God. Thus, my devotion to Him is enabled to become greater. For a small time, at least, I have a taste of celibacy.

Mind you, I don't like it! I definitely don't have the gift for it. But I can appreciate how celibacy is a marvelous gift of God for some people, designed to allow them to make a special contribution to the work of His kingdom.

## (5) Blessing

Finally, the Lord Jesus promised a special blessing for those who forsake the possibilities of a family for His sake. They will be recompensed "a hundred fold" He said (Mark 10:29-30).

That's a pretty good return.

## 15. Masturbation

What does the Bible say about masturbation?

Nothing at all.

This is surprising to many, but it's true. There is no direct scriptural statement about it at all.*

Nevertheless, much that the Bible says is relevant to it and this is what we shall look at now.

First of all, what is masturbation?
It is the handling of one's own sexual organs in such a way as to bring about an orgasm, or sexual climax.

Among young men, it is very common. Few teenage boys have never masturbated. A large

---

*The reference in the King James Bible in 1 Corinthians 6:9 to "abusers of themselves with mankind" is not a reference to masturbation. The Greek words used in the original here are a specific description of homosexuality. Most modern English translations make this clear.

number do so regularly. Among girls, the habit is less common, although on the increase.

Attitudes towards it have varied. The nineteenth century Victorian approach attributed madness, the loss of sexual potency or even the loss of the sex organs themselves to the habit. The twentieth century approach says that the habit is harmless and, in fact, is to be encouraged. Many modern textbooks advocate masturbation as a normal, healthy part of life.

The truth is, as usual, somewhere in between.

There is no evidence of any physical harm from masturbation. But neither should it be encouraged.

Some people have been known to advocate masturbation "under certain conditions." They have argued that if it is solely for the purpose of sexual release, to make sleep or concentration on study easier, then it is no more a sin than taking a cup of coffee or a ham sandwich.

Others have commented that if a young man finds his feelings toward his sweetheart almost impossible to control, it is better to masturbate than to run the risk of committing fornication with her. (Similarly, they assert that within marriage a man may masturbate in order to release sexual pressure, if his wife is unable to have intercourse for some reason.)

However, I would like to point out that the Lord has set up a natural way of releasing sexual tension in young men through nocturnal emissions. Such spontaneous emissions of semen occur during sleep. Many young men, whether they have a sweetheart or not, who masturbate because sexual desire seems too intense, would probably find release if they waited a little longer.

Secondly, masturbation is usually accompanied by sexual fantasies. In other words, during the act the mind is set on thoughts of nudity, intercourse and so on. Many accompany the act by reading "girlie" magazines or other pornographic material. In this case, masturbation is unquestionably sinful. Such thoughts are lustful and unclean. This has been pointed out at considerable length already in earlier pages. To embrace a woman with one's eyes is no different from the act of adultery itself.

When masturbation is accompanied by erotic fantasies, there is no way that it can be considered an innocent act. And the problem is that it is extremely difficult for such fantasies *not* to occur when masturbation is practiced. And thus it becomes sin.

Thirdly, even when masturbation may seem justifiable, it is always only second best. When Paul talks of sexual frustration, he names only marriage as a cure.

"It is better to marry than to be aflame with

passion."
(1 Corinthians 7:9)

Masturbation is not mentioned as an alternative, for masturbation is essentially self-directed. There is no sharing, no giving, no communicating. It is narcisstic. This unusual word means "finding in oneself an object of sexual pleasure." It comes from the legend of Narcissus.

In Greek mythology, Narcissus was a beautiful youth who was passionately loved by the nymph Echo. However, he failed to return her love.

Echo was so grieved that she faded away till only a memory of her voice was left. The god Nemesis punished Narcissus for this by making him fall in love with his own reflection in a pool of water. Of course, the reflection could no more return his love than Narcissus had returned Echo's love. And so, according to the legend, he, too, pined away, and was eventually changed into the narcissus flower.

Hence the term narcissism means self-love. And like Narcissus' love for his own reflection, masturbation is, in the long run, equally unsatisfying. It is joyless sex, for sexual behavior is only really satisfying when it is encased in an act of giving. Sex is to be shared only in the context of commitment. Otherwise, it is but a cheap reflection of the real thing.

Finally, because masturbation is readily available

to the one practicing it, it can become an increasingly difficult habit to break; and a means by which Satan can gain some measure of control over an individual's life, keeping him focused on sex more and more.

For this reason, to the New Testament writers, self-mastery through Jesus is the ideal. If one is not married, then self-control should be exercised.

If you check through the list of the fruit of the Spirit in Galatians 5:22, 23, you will find that the last one named is "self-control." This includes sex. Paul throws down the gauntlet to the lusts of the flesh when he cries:

"I will not be enslaved by anything."
(1 Corinthians 6:12)

The victorious Christian shares the triumph of Paul. He has been liberated by Christ. With God's help, and by the power of the Holy Spirit, he will not be enslaved by anything. There is a joy in such victory—a kind of triumphant exaltation. It is certainly something to praise God for.

Many young people reading this book who want to go on with God and enjoy Christian victory will agree with what I have said. And you are probably already living in a measure of victory. Essentially you are not a slave to sex and you are not bound by masturbation. Nevertheless, it may be that occasionally, in moments of tiredness, or weakness, or frustration, you give in. What normally happens after this is a plunging sense of despair and self-condemnation.

If this does happen, don't be cast down in your spirit. It's not the end of the world! You haven't ruined everything. Granted, you may have disappointed yourself and God. But to mope over it, to live in gloom and shame for days, is worse than the thing itself.

"There is therefore now *no condemnation* for those who are in Christ Jesus."
(Romans 8:1)

These are also the words of Paul. If you do fail, then confess it to God, ask for His forgiveness, and keep going. For if you are in Christ, then you are free from guilt.

To fail may be compared to falling in the mud. To condemn yourself and live in misery over your failure is like staying in the mud. Get up, man! Be cleansed through Jesus Christ, and get going again! You may have slipped, but you don't have to do it again. Believe God for the victory!

You may try to give yourself all kinds of reasons why it's all right to do it "this time." But if you know deep down that it's never all right it will be easier to resist the temptation. No one can make you give in. You do have precious promises by which you can escape corruption. Use them. There is victory for you, if you want it. Be like Paul—refuse to be enslaved by anything!

## 16. Homosexuality
*Some Questions and Answers*

When I was a teenager, I hardly knew what the term "homosexual" meant. And I had never heard of the word "lesbian" at all. Today, even children are being confronted with these terms, and they have become common knowledge.

My two older children were confronted with homosexuals at the age of twelve and ten, respectively. We were attending, of all things, a family kite flying competition. It was hardly the place where one would expect to find homosexuals. But they were there. They came bearing banners and giving out leaflets defending their cause.

I was angry at the invasion. These people had a right to be heard, but they had no right to disrupt a wholesome family day to which people had brought their children in good faith.

Nevertheless, it happened, and I decided to let it be a lesson to my children. So, I engaged in a prolonged discussion with a group of lesbians and a few of my Christians friends, and allowed the children to stay so that they could hear for themselves the issues involved.

I was annoyed that my right as a parent to choose the time for teaching my children about such things had been wrested from me. But as it turned out, it proved a good object lesson for both Rebekah and Michael. Naturally, they had many questions which I tried to answer. The first one was simply, "Daddy, what *is* a homosexual?" This question, and others, I will try to answer here.

*(1) What is a homosexual?*

There are varying degrees of homosexuality. But in simple terms, a homosexual is a person who seeks sexual gratification and satisfaction with a person of his own sex, rather than one of the opposite sex. The term comes from the Greek word *homoios* which means "like." So a *homo*sexual is one who is attracted sexually by those of "like" or similar sex. Most people are *hetero*sexual. This term comes from the Greek word *heteros* which means "other"—i.e. they are attracted by the "other" or opposite sex. Female homosexuals are called *lesbians*. This term is based on the name of the isle of Lesbos, in the Aegean Sea. It is believed that the poetess Sappho, born about 600 B.C., and some of her followers who lived there, were homosexuals. Hence, a female homosexual is known today as a lesbian.

*(2) Are people born homosexuals?*

There is no evidence of inborn or genetic homosexuality.

There are some (usually homosexuals themselves) who claim that the condition is inborn. But this is done in an attempt to escape responsibility.

Then such a person can say, "If I'm born this way, then I can't be blamed for it." Naturally, this avoids any suggestion that homosexuality is a crime, or a sin. If it's inborn, you can't be held responsible. In today's "permissive society," this argument is often readily accepted.

Dr. K. Bockmuhl calls it "the central doctrine of the permissive position." But he goes on to say that this "central doctrine...has been virtually demolished." (*Christianity Today,* 16/2/73, p. 12). In other words, research has shown that there is little evidence for it. In a conversation with me recently, psychologist Dr. John Court claimed that there is, in fact, no evidence for it at all.

Homosexuality is not inborn.

*(3) Is homosexuality abnormal?*

If it is not inborn, is it then abnormal?

Again, there are some who react very strongly against this idea. "Some people are left-handed and some are right-handed," they say, "and some people are homosexuals and some are heterosexuals." But it is not like this at all.

As we have seen, people are not born with homosexual traits.

Furthermore, even on statistics, homosexuality is "abnormal." By this I mean that most people are heterosexual, and if "normal" means "usual or most common," then it is "abnormal" to be otherwise.

Some have claimed that as many as one in four are homosexuals. The famed Kinsey Report, for example, asserted that the percentage of American males who had *at some time* engaged in homosexual activities was of this order. But the report concluded that only one in twenty-five was a practicing homosexual. Therefore, the normal, or most common thing is to be heterosexual.

*(4) How do people become homosexuals, then?*

The reason is often psychological. Textbooks on the subject give a wide variety of possible causes. But they usually stem back to some kind of unsatisfactory home life. I am not qualified to deal with this in detail, nor do I have space here to do so. Furthermore, I am reluctant to give specific examples in case young people who are in such situations feel that they may become homosexuals as a result. It doesn't necessarily follow. For instance, the death or prolonged absence of one parent *may* encourage homosexual tendencies—but it will not necessarily do so. Similarly, distorted relationships with parents, overindulgence by one parent and other similar situations *may* result in homosexuality. But this is still the exception rather than the rule.

A second cause of homosexuality may be environmental. The simple fact of being in a situation where homosexuality flourishes may involve a person. Prisons, army barracks, institutions where people of one sex are thrown together—all of these may expose people to homosexuality, so that they become involved without ever intending to be.

Again, such a situation need not necessarily result in homosexuality—in most cases it probably doesn't. But there are times when it does.

There is a third reason for homosexuality: It is simply human perverseness. Some people are homosexuals because they like being that way. There is no need to look to heredity or environment: the place to look is the human heart. As with many other sins, people do it because they want to do it. This is what Paul meant when he wrote:
"Men likewise gave up natural relations with women and were consumed with passion for one another..."
(Romans 1:27)

*(5) Why does the Bible call homosexual behavior*

## *"unnatural"*?

Homosexuality is "unnatural" because it is contrary to God's plan for sexual relationships. Five times in the Bible these words are quoted:
> "Therefore a man leaves his father and mother and cleaves to his wife, and they become one flesh."
> (Genesis 2:24, Matthew 19:5, Mark 10:7, 1 Corinthians 6:16, Ephesians 5:31)

The original passage in Genesis 2 also says:
> "It is not good that the man should be alone; I will make him a helper fit for him."
> (Genesis 2:18)

Both of these statements teach that sexual union, warm companionship, mutual help and partnership are found in the male-female relationship.

We have already seen how God's plan is for a man and a woman to find satisfaction and companionship on all levels. (Remember the diagrams in Chapter 8?) According to Scripture, there is no better companion for a man than a woman; and no better companion for a woman than a man. The woman was created as a "helper fit for" the man. She was to be the answer to his loneliness. And the reverse is, of course, also true.

There is no room here for a homosexual relationship. In Biblical terms, only a heterosexual relationship is "natural." Other relationships are "unnatural."

This is not to say, of course, that all heterosexual relationships automatically work. This book has shown pretty clearly that very important principles must be applied before an effective partnership can be established. But when a marriage is based on God's Word, it is the best relationship on earth.

The fact that some marriages are unhappy does not mean that the male-female pattern is unsuccessful. Nor does it mean that a homosexual partnership might be better. In fact, very few homosexual relationships last for more than a short time. All it means is that the marriage is not being built according to plan.

One could also add the obvious point that if everyone was a homosexual, it would be self-destructive—no more children would be born. This is another reason why it is "unnatural."

*(6) Are there other reasons why the Bible condemns homosexuality?*

In simple plain terms, the Bible calls homosexuality a sin.

In both 1 Corinthians and 1 Timothy, homosexuality is linked with many other sins such as murder, drunkenness, manslaughter, immorality, adultery, perjury and greed. And the reason why all these things are identified as sin is the same in every case.

All of these sins are essentially selfish. They are all the result of unrestrained desire. They all stem from lack of self-control. They all ignore the needs and rights of others.

In that homosexuality is the result of unbridled passion, it is essentially selfish, and it is thus essentially sinful.

*(7) Was homosexuality in Bible days the same kind of thing as is practiced today?*

I was talking to two clergymen about this one day. We had just witnessed a meeting where there had been considerable "rabbling" and interjection by a group of "gay liberation" people. (Incidentally, here are two words which have been corrupted by homosexuality—what a tragedy that their meanings have been so twisted!)

I began to describe some of the Biblical views on this question, as I have done here. "Oh, no," said one of the men. "I'm sure that today's 'gay' young people have a much more loving and meaningful relationship than the kind of homosexuals the Bible talks about. This is something quite different!"

I was rather stunned by hearing this come from a clergyman. But I was not in a position to argue with him. Since then I have done some reading on the subject. I found that he was completely wrong!

Interestingly, in the Apostle Paul's day homosexuality was regarded more highly by many people than it is today. Consider this: numbered among homosexuals in early times were Plato, Cicero, Seneca, Solon, and Trajan—all renowned men. One writer (Tyrius) claims that of great men of that time only Socrates was exempt from homosexual practice.

Greek plays used homosexuality as themes at times. And most significant of all, some Greek thinkers taught that because of the "superiority" of the male mind, male-to-male relationships would produce a union of minds that would in turn lead to the highest ideology! (See *Barnes' Notes on the N.T.,* Kregel pp. 554 ff.)

Obviously, there was considerable exalted thinking about homosexuality, in some quarters at least. It was certainly not viewed as a degrading thing.

This makes Paul's approach all the more remarkable. In spite of its widespread acceptability, in spite of the fact that many great men were in favor of it, Paul still spoke very strongly against it.

Militant homosexuals claim that the Church today must realize that this is the twentieth century and come to terms with it. They say we must "adapt our moral codes to current social practice."

What would Paul have said if someone had told him to "adapt his moral code to the current social practice"? Probably exactly what he did say:

"Do you not know that the unrighteous will not inherit the kingdom of God? Do not be deceived; neither the immoral ... nor homosexuals ... will inherit the kingdom of God."
(1 Corinthians 6:9-10)

*(8) Can there be such a thing as a homosexual church?*

Recently Troy Perry, founder of a church for homosexuals in Los Angeles, visited Australia. In a newspaper interview he claimed that the needs of "Christian homosexuals" are generally ignored by the established churches. "Part of our purpose," he went on, "is to help homosexuals to come to terms with their homosexuality and to seek God." Homosexuals needed to be "accepted," he said, not rejected.

Undoubtedly, there is some truth in this. Too often churches have rejected, ostracized and ignored homosexuals. Christian people have backed away from them, afraid to touch them "lest they be defiled." This attitude is hypocritical and self-righteous, and decidedly un-Christian. Homosexuals need the same compassion, love and understanding that any other people need.

But you can't just accept them and leave it at that. The gospel of Christ is a transforming thing. It changes people. It destroys their sin and makes them new persons.

It is more than ready to welcome the sinner—*but not his sin.* The sinner must be accepted; the sin must be rejected. Otherwise, the gospel becomes a farce and the church just another club.

A "gay" church is simply an excuse for people who want the fellowship of a church without the responsibility of it. They want a "feeling" of religious acceptance rather than a real relationship with Jesus Christ.

*(9) If a person is a homosexual, is there any reason why he shouldn't be able to express himself sexually in his way seeing that heterosexuals are allowed to express themselves in their way?*

This is a very subtle and plausible argument used by militant homosexuals.

It seems very convincing. But it misses the point.

The fact is that from the Biblical and Christian view, heterosexuals cannot simply express themselves whenever they feel like it. They can only do so through marriage—and even then, there are times when self-control and restraint must be exercised. Apart from marriage, the Biblical standard is chastity and purity.

If they cannot marry, they are expected to be

continually chaste—a fact that has been very strongly emphasised in earlier chapters of this book, I'm sure you will agree.

"Shun immorality," says Paul.
"Do you not know that your body is the temple of the Holy Spirit...so glorify God in your body."
(1 Corinthians 6:18-20)

And remember that Christ Jesus teaches that even looking at a woman for the purpose of lust is sin (Matthew 5:27-28).

Fortunately, for the homosexual there is the promise of total deliverance—even to the removal of the very desire. Sin can be destroyed. Lust can be dealt with. Distorted personalities can be restored. Abnormalities can be made normal.

This is what Jesus meant when he talked about being "born again." Becoming a Christian means starting a new life. Paul put it like this:
"Therefore, if anyone is in Christ, he is a new creation; the old has passed away, behold, the new has come."
(2 Corinthians 5:17)

*(10) What should a homosexual do to overcome his problem?*

First of all, *he must see it as a problem.* Not all homosexuals do. If you are a homosexual, you must face up to the fact that homosexual practice is sin. It is an offense against God. Like pride, greed, drunkenness, hatred, murder, theft, adultery and bitterness, it is wrong.

So the Scripture says:
"Do not be deceived; neither the immoral, nor idolators, nor adulterers, nor homosexuals, nor thieves, nor the greedy, nor drunkards, nor revilers, nor robbers will inherit the kingdom of God."
(1 Corinthians 6:10)

As long as you think homosexuality is okay, you will never be any different. It is better to find out now from Scripture and believe it, than to find out in twenty years time when you are lonely, frustrated, guilty and depressed.

Secondly, *you must believe that it is possible to be delivered from homosexuality*. I have just quoted verse 10 of 1 Corinthians 6. Now look at verse 11:
"And *such were some of you*. But you were *washed*, you were *sanctified*, you were *justified* in the name of the Lord Jesus Christ and in the Spirit of our God."

To be *washed* means to have all the guilt and contamination removed—something which is expressed in believers' baptism.

To be *sanctified* means to be "set apart" from sin. In other words, sin no longer has any hold over you. You have been separated from it. A barrier has been put between you.

To be *justified* means to have all guilt removed. You can stand before God as if you had never sinned at all. Justified is a legal term which means "acquitted" or "pronounced innocent." It is as if God has brought in the verdict of "not guilty."

*The Corinthian Christians had one-time homosexuals among them*. But they were washed, sanctified and justified. The same can be said of you today, if you are or have been a homosexual. Jesus Christ can transform you by the power of His Spirit. Put your faith in Him.

Thirdly, like any other Christian, *a homosexual must learn to exercise self-control*. Even if his past has been dealt with, it is very likely he will be tempted again. Or, as he is now a "normal" person, he will be tempted in a normal fashion by the opposite sex. In either case, he will need to exercise mastery.

So in verse 12, Paul goes on to say: "I will not be enslaved by anything!"

What Paul is saying is this: he is now a servant of Jesus Christ, so he will not be enslaved by *anything* else.

Here is a cry of true liberty. This is real liberation.

"I will not be enslaved by anything!"

This is the freedom cry of the Christian. No longer is he the slave of his passions: through Jesus he is now master. No longer is his behavior determined by his desires: he makes his own decisions.

In spite of the use of terms like "liberation," the homosexual is in fact a slave to passions and desires that he cannot subdue.

He is not his own master. True liberation lies not in being free to do it, but in being free *not* to do it!

In Christ we are truly liberated!

The Apostle Paul speaks often of the power that enables us to live this victorious life in Christ. In Galatians 5:16 he encourages us that if we walk in the Spirit, we *shall not* fulfill the desires of the flesh.

And in this joyful freedom we can join with Paul as he cries:
"I can do *all things* in him who strengthens me!"
(Philippians 4:13)

*(11) What is the Christian attitude towards homosexuals?*

I think this has been covered fairly well already. In summary, however, the Christian attitude can be expressed in these simple terms:

Firstly, *compassion*. Christ gave us the example as He wept with compassion for the sick, the needy and the lost (Matthew 9:35-38).

Secondly, *acceptance*. Homosexuals must be accepted with the same openness as anyone else.

Thirdly, *firmness*. The person may be accepted: *the sin may not.* A homosexual who desires Christian fellowship must be shown that he is welcome, but that by its very nature, the gospel must challenge him to change his ways.

Thus, the attitude shown by Christians to homosexuals must be the same as that shown to any other sinner. For Jesus Christ did not come to call the righteous, but sinners to repentance.

## 17. Famous Last Words

Can I summarize a book like this in a single sentence? Very doubtful!

But I would like to just say this.

The world is full of plausible arguments these days which seem to throw old values into the garbage bin.

As for me, however, I have yet to come across any good reason for discarding the Word of God.

God's Word is unchanging and steadfast. His promises still hold good.

Jesus was not making sweeping statements when he said, "I have come that you might have life—and that you might have it abundantly" (John 10:10).

The thief comes, said Jesus, to steal and kill and destroy. It is the role of the devil to take away our happiness, our peace of mind, our contentedness, indeed our very life! Jesus never came to take away anything worthwhile: He came only to give us the kind of life that God always intended us to have.

You can't lose by living God's way!

If there are any young people reading this who have never established a relationship with Jesus Christ, perhaps you would like to pray now that He might enter your heart. Everything that has been said about the joy and freedom of living the Christian life has been based on having a one-to-one and very personal relationship with Christ, Himself.

In Romans 10:9, Paul shows us the first step in entering this relationship; "If you confess with your lips that Jesus is Lord and believe in your heart that God raised Him from the dead, you will be saved."

So pray this prayer or one similar to it from your heart:
"Lord Jesus, I come before You with a desire to really know You. I believe that You are the Son of God, and that You died and rose again that all of my sins might be forgiven. I accept You as my Lord and Savior. Please come into my heart right now and begin to live Your life through me. Thank You, Jesus. Amen."

I would like to finish with another story. The other

day, a young man came to see me.

"My marriage is on the rocks," he said, sadly. "Finished."

"Is it really so bad, Sam?" I asked. "Surely there is some hope."

"No way," he answered. "I'm not even sure that I want it to succeed anyway. I'd be glad to get out of it."

"Can't I talk to your wife and you together? There must be some way things can be mended."

"Gwen won't talk. She refused point-blank to come with me." (This proved to be quite true—the girl wanted to get out of the marriage. She didn't want anyone talking her back into it!)

"Well, tell me all about it, Sam," I suggested.

So he told me a story of mistake after mistake.

He had with him that day a little three-year-old boy. He was blond, fair-skinned, blue-eyed, with mischievous dimples and a cheeky smile.

Nearly four years previous to this, this little chap had been conceived out of wedlock. Sam was 21 at the time. Gwen was 16. They had only been going together for a couple of months.

When Sam found out that Gwen was pregnant, he felt some sense of responsibility and decided to marry her.

So at the age of 16, Gwen found herself with a husband and, soon, a baby son.

At first everything had been fine. But after the little boy was born things changed. Gwen became cold in her attitude to Sam. Their love-making became boring and dull. Soon they were arguing and fighting.

Sam had a good job. He provided for his wife and his baby son. He remained true to his marriage vows.

But now, after four years of misery, they had broken up. And she, within a few days of the separation, was involved with another man.

Before the separation, they had tried faith in God. But neither had really become very committed.

Now Sam was turning to God for help.

"There have been a lot of mistakes, haven't there, Sam?" I suggested, after he had told me his story.

"There sure have," he agreed.

"First, you engaged in premarital sex. (How often this leads to trouble!) When Gwen became pregnant, you got married. Later, when you tried to follow the Lord, you weren't prepared to really stick to it. All along, you have built on a bad foundation."

"That's it in a nutshell," Sam humbly agreed.

"And Gwen probably blames you for the whole thing—she is resentful that because of you she was deprived of the fun of her later teen years and was saddled with a family well before she should have been."

"How did you know?" asked Sam. "That's almost word for word what she says to me!"

"Well, it's not hard to figure out, Sam," I suggested. "But the point is, what can we do now?"

Well, we prayed about it. I talked to Sam about reconciliation, but even as I talked, there didn't seem much hope.

Then there was the little boy to consider. Arrangements had to be made for him. And so on.

It was a complicated situation and it is still being worked out.

The one bright spot is Sam's own personal spiritual life. He has turned back to God and everything is different for him. He has a joy and a confidence about him that is surprising.

But what sadness and tragedy he has been through!

All because in the teenage years, when foundations are laid and directions established, he made some fundamental mistakes.

I hope that you will do better. My prayer is that this book will be used by God to help you—and many other young people—to build strong foundations and plot careful routes through life.

God's Word says that even a fool can't go wrong when he follows the highway of holiness (Isaiah 35:8). I don't know about you, but I find that very reassuring!

So remember, God's divine power has granted to us all things that pertain to life and godliness... by which He has granted to us His precious and very great promises (in the Bible), that through these we may *escape the corruption that is in the world because of passion*—and become partakers of God's divine nature!

So take hold of His promises and make your way safely through life!

I know you can do it!

God bless you as you go.

# 18. Things You Probably Want To Know

Here is a list of questions that young people often ask. The answers occur somewhere in this book. So page references are given after each question telling you where to find them:

Page

1. Does it matter how a girl dresses?   15-23, 58

2. Is it all right to express sexual desires if you have them?   25-27

3. What effect does thought life have on sexual behavior?   31-36, 117-119

4. Are males and females attracted to each other for the same reasons?   27-29

5. Why should teenagers have to control their sexual urges when married people don't have to?   31-36, 122-123

|     |                                                                                | Page                      |
| --- | ------------------------------------------------------------------------------ | ------------------------- |
| 6.  | How is it possible to control sexual urges?                                    | 31-36, 117-124            |
| 7.  | Is it all right to do something if everyone else does it?                      | 37-41, 48                 |
| 8.  | What is love?                                                                  | 44-48, 87-89, 135-136     |
| 9.  | What are some of the "lines" that girls should watch out for?                  | 43-56                     |
| 10. | What are some of the "lines" fellows should watch out for?                     | 56-59                     |
| 11. | What if my sexual attitudes make me unpopular?                                 | 37-41, 48                 |
| 12. | What do I do if my boyfriend expects me to show him my love by having sex?     | 47-48                     |
| 13. | Is it OK to have sex if you're going to get married anyway?                    | 48-53                     |
| 14. | What is fornication?                                                           | 39, 52                    |
| 15. | What does it mean to be "frigid"?                                              | 53-54                     |

|     |                                                                               | Page              |
| --- | ----------------------------------------------------------------------------- | ----------------- |
| 16. | Is sexual prowess a sign of manliness?                                        | 56-57             |
| 17. | Is it dangerous to be sexually aroused without fulfillment?                   | 57-58             |
| 18. | If a girl isn't looking for trouble, she'll probably be all right, won't she? | 61-64             |
| 19. | How can I avoid getting into a situation where I could be sexually involved?  | 61-64             |
| 20. | If sex is fun, what's wrong with having fun?                                  | 65-103            |
| 21. | What is there to be ashamed of in sex?                                        | 67-68             |
| 22. | What sort of things should I look for in the person I marry?                  | 68-73             |
| 23. | Is it all right for a Christian to marry a non-Christian?                     | 70-71             |
| 24. | What is the best basis for marriage?                                          | 75-84             |
| 25. | What is the most important aspect of marriage?                                | 77-82,<br>124-126 |

|     |                                                                                                                                                 | Page            |
| --- | ----------------------------------------------------------------------------------------------------------------------------------------------- | --------------- |
| 26. | If two people love each other, what difference does it make whether they have a legal wedding or not? It's only a bit of paper.                 | 76-84           |
| 27. | How important is sex in marriage?                                                                                                               | 85-86, 128-136  |
| 28. | When sexual intercourse takes place, does the woman reach a climax at the same time as the man?                                                 | 88-89           |
| 29. | Why is it so important to wait until marriage before having sex?                                                                                | 67-68, 82-89    |
| 30. | Does the enjoyment of sex decrease over the years?                                                                                              | 89-92           |
| 31. | Now that the "pill" is so easily available, and it is possible to avoid pregnancy, what's wrong with premarital sex?                            | 92-98           |
| 32. | Is abortion the "easy way out"?                                                                                                                 | 93-96           |
| 33. | Is it all right to marry if you don't intend to have children?                                                                                  | 92-98           |
| 34. | Is venereal disease still a danger?                                                                                                             | 100-102         |

|     |                                                                     | Page             |
| --- | ------------------------------------------------------------------- | ---------------- |
| 35. | How far has medical science controlled V.D.?                        | 100-101          |
| 36. | Can V.D. be fatal?                                                  | 101              |
| 37. | How can you stop having sex if you like it?                         | 102-103          |
| 38. | Is it the girl's responsibility to say "no"?                        | 105-108          |
| 39. | How far can a couple go?                                            | 105-108          |
| 40. | What does the saying mean, "Be sure your sin will find you out"?    | 108-109          |
| 41. | If you have failed in the past, what can you do about it?           | 115-116, 146-147 |
| 42. | Is it wrong to see R- and X-rated films?                            | 117-119          |
| 43. | What is a Christian?                                                | 119-122          |
| 44. | How can I help it if temptation gets too much for me?               | 120-121          |
| 45. | Is it wrong to experience sexual desires?                           | 122              |

|     |                                                           | Page         |
| --- | --------------------------------------------------------- | ------------ |
| 46. | How often can you have sex in marriage?                   | 122-123      |
| 47. | What is fasting?                                          | 124          |
| 48. | What is the most important factor in a happy sex relationship? | 125-126 |
| 49. | What is the purpose of sex?                               | 128-136      |
| 50. | What rights have husband and wife over each other?        | 128-129      |
| 51. | Is it a sin to enjoy sex?                                 | 130-133      |
| 52. | Does the Bible speak openly about sex?                    | 128-133      |
| 53. | Does sex improve your understanding of your husband or wife? | 133-134   |
| 54. | What is celibacy?                                         | 137-141      |
| 55. | Are there any good reasons for not marrying?              | 137-141      |
| 56. | Is it all right for a married couple to be separated occasionally? | 122-123, 140 |
| 57. | What is masturbation?                                     | 142-147      |

|     |                                                      | Page    |
| --- | ---------------------------------------------------- | ------- |
| 58. | Is masturbation wrong?                               | 142-147 |
| 59. | How can masturbation be overcome?                    | 146-147 |
| 60. | What is a homosexual? What is a lesbian?             | 149     |
| 61. | Are people born as homosexuals?                      | 150     |
| 62. | How do people become homosexuals?                    | 150-152 |
| 63. | What's wrong with homosexuality?                     | 152-163 |
| 64. | Can a Christian be a homosexual?                     | 157-158 |
| 65. | What is the Christian attitude towards homosexuals?  | 162-163 |